Candles

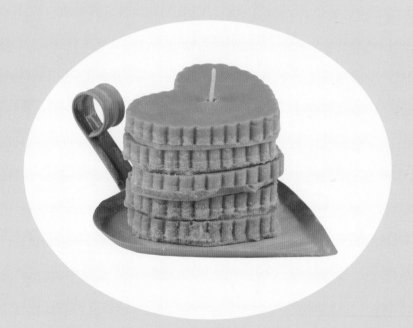

ELAINE STAVERT

Candles

GUILD OF MASTER CRAFTSMAN PUBLICATIONS

A worker bee.

Unrefined beeswax.

Refining beeswax

The only beeswax refinery now operating in the UK is the British Wax Refining Company Ltd, founded in 1914 by Sidney Charles Case-Green. This company's beeswax is sourced from around the world so can differ in colour depending on the country of origin and method of melting at source. In order to use beeswax for its numerous applications, it needs to be refined (cleaned) to remove any impurities.

Applications such as creams and balms require white beeswax. This is produced by various methods of bleaching. To make refined beeswax into easily usable granules, it is frozen and then passed through a granulating machine.

British Wax has a long history of refining and processing natural waxes. The story began when Sidney Charles Case-Green joined the Beeswax Company Ltd of Liverpool in 1899 where he gained his expert knowledge of waxes. Sidney then founded his own company for the purpose of bleaching and refining wax. Under the leadership of Sidney's sons the business grew as they supplied companies such as the famous London wax figure museum, Madame Tussauds, whom they still supply to this day. The family tradition continued with Sidney's grandsons and is now run by his great grandchildren who continue to seek and develop new applications for wax.

Soya wax

Soya (or soy in the US) is a native East Asian plant that has been grown in China since records began. Introduced into the US in the 19th century, it is now one of its leading crops, grown extensively in Illinois, Iowa and Indiana. Soya has had many uses: soy sauce, coffee substitute and as a fertilizer for crops. Due to its high protein content, it is used to make soya milk and tofu. It is also used for cattle food and as a bio-fuel.

How is soya made into wax?

To make soya wax, the soya beans are harvested and processed into oil, which is then purified and hydrogenated. This turns most of the unsaturated fatty acids into saturated fat, producing a solid creamy-white wax, which is available in flake or pellet form.

An eco-friendly choice

Soya is an eco-friendly choice being both renewable and biodegradable. Kosher and vegan-friendly, it also produces a cleaner, longer burn than paraffin (up to twice as long) due to its low melting temperature. Spillages can be cleaned up with hot soapy water. Some scientists claim that inhaled emissions from paraffin candles after long-term use, or in confined spaces, may increase the risks of cancer and asthma. It has been reported that neither beeswax nor soya candles emit such toxic chemicals.

Other soya producers include Brazil, Argentina, Paraguay, China and India. However, environmentalists are worried that Brazilian crops are causing deforestation of their rainforests. Happily, most of the soya waxes available are made from sustainable pesticide-free crops grown in the US, but you could check with your supplier to make sure that your soya wax comes from ethical sources.

A huge range of products can be made from the soya bean.

Soya wax candles.

Basic techniques

Equipment and basic steps

To make the recipes in this book you will not need any complicated equipment; most of the things that you need will probably be in your kitchen already. You will, however, need to purchase the ingredients to make your candles.

These are easily obtained from mail order candlemaking suppliers or high street craft shops (see our list of suppliers on pages 150–151). Here are some of the ingredients and equipment you will need for candlemaking.

Apron – to protect your clothing from splashes of wax, fragrance or colour

Baking tray – either for use with cookie cutter candles, or in which to place your mould in case of wax leakage

Candle wax (1) – soya container wax, soya pillar wax, beeswax blocks or beeswax sheets (see page 25)

Colour (2) – candle dye to add to the melted wax (see page 37)

Cooking timer – you may wish to set your timer to alert you when your wax may be melted. With experience you will have more of an idea of how long wax takes to melt

Decoration (3) – appliqué wax, transfers and bronzing powders (see pages 61–64)

Dipping container (4) – a tall thin metal container made specially for making dipped candles

2

1

3

Double boiler (5) – or a bowl, small saucepan or metal dish placed over, or in, a saucepan of simmering water. You could also use a clean tin can with the side pinched to make a pouring spout. Alternatively use a crock-pot, electric casserole, stew pot or a professional larger-sized wax melter

Eye goggles – to protect your eyes from splashes of wax

Fragrance or essential oils (6) – candle fragrance oil that is formulated specially for candles or essential (aromatherapy) oils (see pages 38–39)

Hairdryer or heat gun – gently heating with a hairdryer or heat gun can briefly warm the wax and smooth away any unwanted scratches on the surface of a candle

Kitchen foil or greaseproof/wax paper – you may wish to cover your surfaces to protect them from wax. You can also cover your cooker hob with kitchen foil to avoid wax spills but remember that this may get hot. Soya wax can be cleaned up with hot soapy water

Kitchen scales – if you are measuring your wax and fragrance by weight

Knife – for cutting sheets of beeswax

Ladle – metal or durable plastic for ladling wax into moulds if not using a pouring jug

4

5

6

Measuring jug – made of metal, heat-resistant glass or durable plastic for measuring out liquid wax if using liquid measurements

Metal jug (7) – with pouring lip, for melting wax directly on a cooker hob (and useful for melting small amounts of wax)

Mould (8) – metal, plastic, rubber, silicone, container, preserve jar, milk carton, any container that is heatproof and non-flammable. Cookie cutters for cut-out candles (see pages 26–29)

Mould seal (9) – a type of putty used to seal the hole around the wick on the base of moulds to prevent wax from seeping out. You could also use modelling clay or Blu-Tack®

Oven gloves – handles can get hot when melting wax

Scissors – for cutting wicks

Spoon – made of plastic or wood. Plastic is best as it will not absorb as much fragrance as a wooden spoon

Thermometer (10) – a wax, sugar or digital thermometer

Warning labels – if you are selling candles or even just giving them away as a present you must always provide a warning label with safety instructions for burning candles (see page 69). Make your own labels or buy ready-made stickers to affix to your final candle

Wax glue (11) – a sticky wax for placing on the bottom of tabbed wicks to fix them to the bottom of moulds to help keep them in place. A hot glue gun can be used in place of wax glue, or glue dots can also be purchased

Wick (12) – there are various types of wick available to suit different types of candles (see pages 30–32)

Wicking needle – a large needle that enables you to wick your rubber or silicone moulds

Wick supports/sustainers/bars (13) – small wooden sticks to hold your wicks in place. These include kebab sticks, barbecue sticks, chopsticks, pencils or cocktail sticks bound at each end with rubber bands, lollipop/popsicle or metal wick bars from candle suppliers

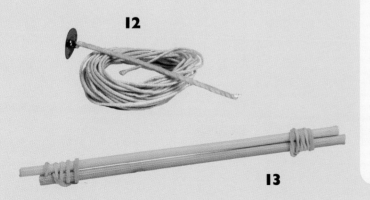

12

13

Basic steps

A candle is essentially melted wax with the addition of fragrance, colour and a wick to light and burn the candle. The steps below show the basic process of how to make your own candles using this book.

1 Decide on a theme and type for the candle (see page 24)

2 Select your type of wax and mould or container (see pages 25–29)

3 Decide on the type and size of wick you are going to use (see pages 30–32)

4 Measure/weigh the wax (see page 34)

5 Melt the wax and add the colour, candle fragrance or essential oils (see pages 35–39)

6 Wick the candle and pour the wax according to the individual candlemaking techniques (see pages 40–60)

7 Test burn the candle and pay attention to fire safety rules and candle burning tips (see pages 65–71)

Types of candle

What do you want to achieve from your candle? Is it for relaxation at the end of the day? Is it for soft lighting at a dinner party? Or is it simply to repel insects at a picnic?

Deciding on a theme for your candle should help you select the type of candle to make. For instance, for a relaxing aroma you could use essential oils in a container candle to achieve a good scent throw; dipped candles make an attractive dinner table arrangement or little votive candles with lemongrass may keep the wasps away from your jam sandwiches. The information on the following pages will help you further in your choice of candle.

Dipped candle
(See page 50)

Beeswax rolled candle
(See page 52)

Container candle
(See page 46)

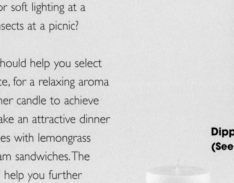

Pillar candle
(See page 40)

Cookie cutter candle
(See page 57)

Tea lights
(See page 49)

Floating candle
(See page 56)

Votive candle
(See page 45)

Types of wax

Soya pillar blend wax

This wax is a creamy white colour and comes in flake form. It is specially blended for candles that stand up on their own i.e. pillar or moulded candles. Pillars, votives, wax tarts and aroma melts are all made with soya pillar wax. Two pours are often needed for this type of candle as the wax can shrink leaving voids on the top of the candle.

Soya wax melts at a low temperature and is therefore not suitable for tapers, dining candles or pillar candles of less than 2½in (6.5cm) as the candle will drip. Soya wax can easily be cleaned up with hot soapy water.

Soya container wax

This wax is a creamy white colour and comes in flake form. It is specially blended for use in containers and cannot be used for freestanding candles. It has a low melting point and quickly becomes liquid when lit, creating a large 'burn pool' (area of melted wax). As the wax melts, the fragrance in the melted wax is released into the room.

Some brands of soya container wax offer several different blends of wax. Some are more resistant to frosting or 'bloom' (chalky white crystals) and are more suitable for coloured candles. Other blends have a better adhesion to containers and are best uncoloured. Read your supplier's information on each wax before making a decision.

Beeswax

Beeswax is obtained from the cappings of the honeycomb and in its raw state has the most delicious honey-like smell. Beeswax is expensive and luxurious and can be used for all types of candle. However, it works particularly well for dipped candles and for latex rubber or silicone moulds.

Beeswax comes in the form of yellow pellets or blocks that retain all of the wonderful honey scent. Unfragranced, or deodorized bleached white beeswax pellets can be purchased if you wish to add scent and colour to your beeswax candle, or you can refine the wax from your own beehives.

Note: Beeswax can also be used for making container candles, however I would recommend soya container wax as a first choice.

A beeswax block. In tray from left to right: soya pillar blend, white beeswax pellets and soya container wax.

Moulds and containers

Metal pillar moulds

These are the best and most durable moulds to use, but they can be expensive. Metal moulds are usually seamless to give a good crisp finish to your candle. They are generally available in round, square, octagon and star shapes. Soya pillar blend wax or beeswax is used with these moulds. The moulds can last for many years and should be a good investment.

Containers

The advantage of making a container candle is that the container is also the mould and any liquid wax remains inside the container. This also helps to protect your carpets and furniture from wax spillage.

Soya container wax is poured directly into heat-resistant containers such as storage jars, plant pots, garden urns, apothecary jars, preserve jars, tea lights, metal tins, old tin cans, glass containers (as long as they are thick enough or heat proof), shells, silver pots and metal buckets. Make sure that your containers are clean and free from debris.

Polycarbonate or plastic moulds

These moulds come in interesting shapes such as hearts, eggs, rounds, pyramids and pentagons as well as round and square pillars. You can also buy polycarbonate or plastic moulds with several impressions on one sheet for making votives or floating candles. Long-term use of essential oils or fragrance may damage polycarbonate or plastic moulds. You may get a seam of wax if using a two-part mould but this can easily be removed with a knife.

Other moulds

Providing that your wax is not poured at too high
a temperature, plastic, metal, rubber or cardboard items
from around the house can be used as moulds. Look
around your home for suitable items such as margarine
tubs, yoghurt pots, plastic drawer tidies, cardboard boxes,
empty popcorn buckets, potato chip/crisp tubes, food
storage tubs, tin cans, empty sweet or candy tins, biscuit
tins, milk or juice cartons.

Sand candle moulds

An impression is made in damp sand and the void
filled with soya pillar blend wax or beeswax. See
page 53 for full instructions.

A sand candle 'mould'.

Latex rubber and silicone moulds

These moulds are often used to create intricate designs, interesting textures or unusual shapes. A whole host of amazing rubber or silicone moulds are available from intricate flowers, fruits, beehives and animals, to dinner candles and interestingly shaped pillar moulds. Most beekeeping suppliers usually have a good range of these type of moulds – see the list of suppliers on pages 150–151. When using beeswax for moulded or pillar candles you will need to spray your mould first with silicone spray or vegetable oil for easy release.

These moulds will require a wicking needle so that you can make a hole in the rubber through which to thread the wick. Use beeswax with these moulds, or you can use soya pillar blend wax as long as the diameter of the soya candle is a minimum of 2½–3in (6.5–7.5cm) so that a ½in (1cm) wall is created in the first inch of burning to prevent wax leakage.

Preparing moulds

Soya wax should be self-releasing. If the soya wax does stick to your mould, or if you are using beeswax, you can use silicone spray or vegetable oil to coat your mould first for easy release. Always check your moulds for scratches as any marks will leave an impression on the candle.

Cleaning moulds

There is no need to wash your moulds unless they are particularly dirty or smelling strongly of fragrance. Wash them with warm soapy water.

Making latex rubber moulds

You can easily make your own moulds at home using latex liquid rubber. It is particularly good for getting into little crevices and for picking up intricate details and texture. Have a look around the home or in the natural world for interesting objects such as citrus fruits or pine cones.

1 You can either paint the liquid latex on to the object (stand it on an upturned mug or bowl), or dip it straight into the liquid latex.

2 If the crevices are particularly deep, dipping is recommended.

3 Leave each layer to set slightly before applying the next and keep building them up. This may take quite a few dips, but you can also use latex rubber gel, which is thicker than the liquid and will build up the thickness more quickly. However, the latex is surprisingly strong and you will often only need to create a thickness of a few millimetres.

4 Leave the mould to set overnight and gently peel the rubber away from the object. Use your homemade mould to make a candle in the same way as you would with any other rubber mould (see page 42).

Selecting a wick

What is a wick?

A wick is a specially made combination of braided cotton plies, or wood, set within a candle. It consumes melted wax like fuel to keep the flame burning. To achieve the best burn, choosing the right wick is the most important part of candlemaking.

If the wick is too small it will not draw up enough melted wax and the candle can drip. If the wick is too big, the candle could burn too quickly causing smoke or mushrooming (see troubleshooting on pages 70–71). By choosing the correct wick, your candle should consume all of the wax at the right pace, with no dripping, and should produce a good steady flame approximately 1in (2.5cm) high.

Each type and size of candle, blend and brand of wax, fragrance, essential oil, colour and wick will react differently with each other. As each combination of these factors is unique, it is impossible to indicate the exact wick to use in your candle. Only by test burning (see pages 65–67) will you find the best wick for your candle.

However, the wick guide on page 32 gives you suggested starting points for wick testing. These are recommendations only and are not limited to the wicks suggested. You should always fully test burn a candle to find the most suitable wick.

Types of wick

Only 'candle' wicks should be used in candles. Never use string, twine, rope or sticks. They may look similar, but wicks have been developed to burn safely. Modern wicks curl over slightly at the tip so that the carbon burns off and does not build up or mushroom. Using anything that is not a candle wick is a fire hazard. Always trim wicks to ¼in (0.5cm) before burning.

There are many types of wick available, however, not all are suitable for use in beeswax or soya wax candles. Below and opposite are some of the recommended wicks to use.

Flat-braided wicks – LX series

A self-trimming thin, flat wick that curls into the flame minimizing carbon build-up or mushrooming. This wick helps to centralize the heat, preventing overheating of containers and tunnelling in pillar candles. Use these wicks with soya wax.

ECO multipurpose wick series

A flat, coreless cotton wick with thin interwoven paper filaments/threads providing a controlled self-trimming effect, which reduces mushrooming, soot and smoke. Use these wicks with soya wax.

Tea light wicks – TL wick series

A tightly braided non-cored flat wick designed for tea lights and small candles. Self-trimming with a slight curl, minimizing carbon build up or mushrooming. It provides a controlled flame with greater safety in metal and plastic tea light cups. Use these wicks with soya wax.

Wood wicks

Provide the soft crackling sound of a wood fire. The amount of crackle that you get from your candle may depend on the reaction between your fragrance and colour, the more you use, the more your candle may crackle. Trim the wick before burning and light the whole of the wick. These wicks are for use with natural waxes.

Square-braided wicks

Bleached cotton wicks for use with moulded, pillar and dipped beeswax candles. Designed to curl slightly as the candle burns to avoid carbon build-up and mushrooming. Use these wicks with beeswax.

Cored wicks

You may see wicks with metal, paper or cotton cores for sale. However, these are not recommended for use with soya candles.

A selection of wicks, from left to right: unwaxed wick, pre-waxed cut wicks, wooden wicks and pre-tabbed waxed wicks.

Wick guide

These wick recommendations are suggestions only and you may wish to try other types or sizes of wick. If you have a pillar candle that is an uneven shape, take the average diameter from the middle of the candle to work out wick size.

Candle diameter (in)	Candle diameter (mm)	Wick suggestions for initial burn testing
Soya container candles		
Tea light (or tiny container)	Tea light (or tiny container)	TL10, TL13, TL15, TL18, TL21, TL25, TL28, TL31
1–2in	25–50mm	LX8, LX10, ECO0.5, ECO1, ECO2
2–2½in	50–65mm	LX12, LX14, ECO1, ECO2, ECO4, ECO5
2½–3in	65–75mm	LX14, LX16, LX18, ECO4, ECO5, ECO6, ECO8, ECO10
3–3½in	75–90mm	LX18, LX20, LX22, LX24, LX28, ECO10, ECO12, ECO14
3½–4in	90–100mm	LX26, LX28, LX30, ECO14, ECO16
4in plus	100mm plus	You will need to use two or more evenly spaced wicks
Soya pillar candles		
Votive	Votive	LX10, LX12, LX14, ECO1, ECO2, ECO4
2–2½in	50–65mm	LX12, LX14, ECO1, ECO2, ECO4, ECO5
2½–3in	65–75mm	LX14, LX16, LX18, ECO4, ECO5, ECO6, ECO8, ECO10
3–3½in	75–90mm	LX18, LX20, LX22, LX24, LX28, ECO10, ECO12, ECO14
3½–4in	90–100mm	LX26, LX28, LX30, ECO14, ECO16
4in plus	100mm plus	You will need to use two or more evenly spaced wicks
Beeswax candles – NT wicks		
Votive	Votive	NT29, NT32, NT35
Tea lights/small candles 1–2in	Tea lights/small candles 25–45mm	NT20, NT23, NT26
1½–2⅛in	35–55mm	NT29, NT32, NT35
2–2½in	45–65mm	NT38, NT41, NT44, NT47
2½–3in	60–75mm	NT53, NT59
3–3½in	75–90mm	NT65, NT71
Beeswax candles – square-braided wicks		
¼in	6mm	No.0
½in	13mm	No.1
¾in	19mm	No.1A
1in	25mm	No.2
1¼in	32mm	No.3
1½in	38mm	No.4
1¾in	45mm	No.5
2in	50mm	No.6
2½in	65mm	No.7
4in	100mm	No.8
Wood wicks		
2in	50mm	Small
2¾–3⅛in	70–80mm	Medium
4in	100mm	Large

Purchasing and preparing your wick

Once you have selected your wick size and type, choose the length required – wick can be purchased by the roll or pre-cut. Measure the length of your mould and select a wick that is 1–2in (2.5–5cm) longer so that it can easily be tied or held in place with wick sustainers. It is better to select more wick than needed and cut off the excess when the candle is set, than to be short.

Priming a wick

For all recipes you will need a primed wick. This is simply a wick that has been dipped and coated in wax. Priming a wick aids the initial lighting of your candle. It will also stiffen the it, helping it to stand up in container candles and will make it easier to thread through holes in moulded candles. You can either prime your own wick, following the instructions below, or you can purchase them ready-primed.

Tabbed wicks

If you are making a container candle, consider using a 'tabbed wick' (a wick with a round metal tab fixed to one end). Place a piece of glue to the base of the metal tab and secure it to the bottom of your container, this will help to keep the wick in place. You can purchase pre-tabbed waxed (primed) wicks in different lengths or you can buy the tabs separately, affix to the bottom of your primed wick, and crimp the ends to secure.

1 To prime your own wick first dip the wick in liquid wax to coat it.

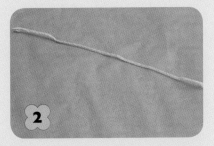

2 Leave the wick lying in a straight line on a piece of greaseproof or wax paper for a few minutes until set. The only exception to this rule is for dipped candles. By the very nature of the dipping process you are effectively priming your candle with the first dip.

Important
Make sure that you wick your candle appropriately for the type of candle you are making. See pages 40–60 to find out how to wick individual types of candles.

Basic method

Measuring and weighing wax

Method one
Calculate the amount of liquid wax needed:
Fill the mould with water (block any holes with mould seal), pour the water into a measuring jug and measure the liquid, use the same amount of liquid wax.

Method two
Calculate the weight of unmelted wax needed:
Fill the mould with water (block any holes with mould seal). Pour the water into a measuring jug and measure the liquid. Water weighs approximately the same as its liquid measurement (i.e. 1 litre of water = 1kg of water), however wax weighs 15 per cent less. So, divide the liquid water measurement measure by 1.15. For example:

measurement of water = 150ml ÷ 1.15
= 4.5oz (130g) unmelted wax

Method three
Measure the proportional size of the container to the wax:
Using wax flakes or pellets, measure 1½ times the size of the container, i.e. for a one cup container use 1½ cups of wax.

It is always best to overestimate the amount of wax needed as it is difficult to quickly melt, fragrance and colour more wax if you are short whilst at a crucial stage of making. You may also need extra wax for a second pouring of pillar candles. Any leftover wax can always be kept and re-used.

Conversion table of water to weight of wax

Water (ml) (or ml of liquid wax)	= Weight of unmelted wax (oz)	= Weight of unmelted wax (g)
50ml	= 1.5oz	= 43g
100ml	= 3oz	= 85g
150ml	= 4.5oz	= 130g
200ml	= 6oz	= 175g
300ml	= 9oz	= 260g
400ml	= 12oz	= 350g
500ml	= 15oz	= 425g
1 litre	= 30oz	= 850g

Melting wax

Set the cooking timer for 20 minutes so that you do not forget the melting wax. Use a double boiler (one pan sits half inside the other, which is filled with simmering water). This provides a gentle heat underneath. All beeswax should be heated this way. You could also use a heat-resistant glass or metal jug, or a bowl placed over a saucepan of water.

1 Turn on the heat source for the melting pot and gently melt the wax in the double boiler. **Do not** leave melting wax unattended at any time as wax can combust.

2 Make sure that the water in the double boiler does not boil dry. After 20 minutes check that the wax has melted.

Alternative ways of heating wax

If you are extremely careful you can heat the soya wax (not beeswax) in a metal container directly on the cooker hob, but you must make sure that the wax is heated up very gently and doesn't overheat.

Another idea is to melt the wax in an electric casserole dish or stew pot/crock-pot. Professional pots and melters can also be purchased – see the suppliers list on pages 150–151.

Metal pot

Professional melter

Wax melting and pouring

Use the following wax temperature table to heat the wax to the required temperature. **Never heat your wax above 200°F (93°C).** Not only can high temperatures be extremely dangerous, but heating the wax too high can cause the wax to discolour and may affect the burn quality of the candle. The wax should melt fairly quickly so always stay in the room while the wax is melting, set your cooking timer if you are forgetful. Test the temperature with a cooking thermometer, dip it into the wax and immediately wipe off the wax with some kitchen roll, or use a digital thermometer. If adding powdered dye, heat the wax to 190°F (87°C) so that the powder completely dissolves.

Wax melting temperatures

Type of wax	Melting temperature	Melting temperature if using powder dye	Pouring temperature
Container blend (containers and tea lights)	155°F (68°C)	190°F (87°C)	125°F (51°C) 155°F (63°C) (tall, thin jars)
Pillar blend (pillars, moulded, votives, tarts)	165°F (73°C)	190°F (87°C)	1st pour 155°F (63°C) 2nd pour 145°F (62°C)
Beeswax (pillars, moulded, votives)	165°F (73°C)	190°F (87°C)	155°F (68°C)

Important

This table is a guide only and you should refer to your manufacturer's instructions, or supplier's details, for specific instructions on melting your wax as each brand of wax may require slightly different melting and pouring temperatures. You can pour as low as 100°F (37°C) as long as you keep stirring the wax.

Thermometer

Adding the colour

Liquid, chip and block dyes can all be added to wax at 155°F (68°C) and at 190°F (87°C) for powder dyes. Pre-coloured beeswax blocks can also be purchased. Colour can fade in the light and UV inhibitors can be purchased to add to the wax to help prevent colour loss.

1 Heat the wax to the required temperature and add the colour.

2 Stir thoroughly until it is completely dissolved. Candle colour tends to be fairly concentrated so only add a little to start with; you can always add more. Melted candle wax will always look much darker than the set wax, which will set much paler.

3 To get an idea of the colour that the candle will be when set, spoon a little coloured candle wax on to a piece of greaseproof paper or on to a plastic tray, leave for a few minutes until set, if the colour is too pale simply add more colour to the melting pot.

Adding the candle fragrance or essential oil

It is very important that you only use a fragrance that is sold as a candle fragrance oil. For instance, a soap-making or potpourri fragrance may actually be dangerous to use in a candle. This is because the flash point (the point at which it catches fire) could be too high as the fragrance may contain alcohol.

An 'apple pie' fragrance from one company could be made with different ingredients from a fragrance with the same name from another company. Remember to ask your supplier if any of their fragrances have been tested with the brand of wax that you are using.

If a fragrance is not compatible with your candle, it can cause the wax to sweat, frost or bloom, it may create a small burn pool or poor scent throw, it could also cause an inferior burn with mushroom or sooting, a lumpy surface or bad adhesion to the sides of a container candle. If your candle experiences any of these symptoms it could be the type of fragrance that you are using and you may wish to try a similar fragrance from another supplier. However, it could also be the wrong choice of wick, or the pouring temperature that is causing one of these problems, so it may be a good idea to try another wick or pouring temperature before purchasing a different candle fragrance oil. You could also try re-making your candle using less of the candle fragrance oil.

Essential oils (aromatherapy oils from plants) can also be used for their wonderful aromas and therapeutic scents, and again testing for suitability in your candle is important. Refer to the section on essential oils on pages 74–80 for further information. Before buying large quantities of fragrance, always make sure that you have fully test-burned your candles (see pages 65–67).

Adding the essential oil or fragrance

1   Add the fragrance or essential oil last to prevent evaporation and so the essential oils do not lose any of their therapeutic properties. Adding the fragrance may cool the wax slightly.

2   Make sure that you stir in your fragrance or essential oil thoroughly into the melted wax.

Amount of scent to use

The recommended amount of fragrance to use in candles is up to 10 per cent for candle fragrance oils and up to 5 per cent for essential oils. This means that for 5 per cent you should use 5ml (or 1 teaspoon) per 100ml of liquid wax.

If you are making candles professionally, it is best to work out the amounts of fragrance by weight as large amounts are sold in this way. This is because some essential oils weigh more than others. Weigh the amount of liquid fragrance/essential oils. Five per cent of 100g (3½oz) = 5g (0.18oz), etc.

For all of the recipes in this book we have used approximately 5 per cent fragrance or essential oils. Essential oils can be expensive so you can always use less than the amount specified in the recipes to save on costs, or use a fragrance oil instead (fragrance oils are cheaper than essential oils). Or, if you wish to have a more strongly scented candle you will need to increase the amount of candle fragrance oil (not essential oils) to a maximum of 10 per cent. However, by increasing the fragrance levels you take the risk of possibly reducing the burn quality of your candle.

Pouring the wax

When the coloured and fragranced wax is at the desired temperature, gently pour it into the mould. If you have a melting pot without a spout, you may find it easier to ladle the wax into the mould with a plastic or metal ladle.

If you are making container candles, the containers should be at room temperature. If they are very cold, you may wish to gently heat them up in the oven or warm them with a hairdryer. Containers and moulds should be placed at least ½in (1.5cm) apart so that air can circulate freely between each candle.

Candles should not be cooled too quickly, the temperature of your room should be around 70°F (21°C). The candle should now be left undisturbed to set for at least 48 hours.

Caution: If you have excess wax, pour it into a yoghurt pot or plastic container for re-use. Never pour melted wax down the drain. It will solidify and block the drain.

Types of candlemaking

Pillar and moulded candles

Both pillar and moulded candles are freestanding candles that are made in moulds (metal, polycarbonate, plastic, rubber or silicone, or sand) using either beeswax or a special soya pillar wax. As the first inch (2.5cm) of a pillar candle burns down, a wall of wax should occur around the sides of the candle, this wall keeps the liquid wax contained.

As well as beeswax, soya pillar blend wax can be used to make pillar moulds as long as the diameter of the soya pillar is minimum of 2½–3in (6.5–7.5cm) so that the wall can occur during burning to prevent wax leakage. If you are using beeswax, spray your mould with silicone mould release or coat it with vegetable oil to make unmoulding easier.

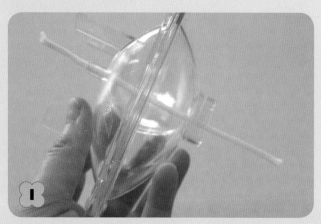

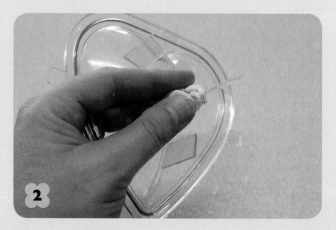

1 Take a primed wick (see page 33) and feed the wick through the holes in the mould.

2 Seal with mould seal, modelling clay or Blu-Tack to prevent any liquid wax from escaping.

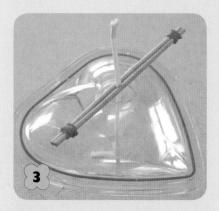

3 Place the other end of the wick between the two sticks of the wick sustainer and pull gently so that the wick is taut and centrally positioned in the mould (otherwise the candle will burn unevenly). If you do not have wick sustainers you could tie the end of a wick to a skewer or chopstick – you will need to cut a slightly longer piece of wick to allow for this.

4 Melt, colour and fragrance the soya pillar wax or beeswax and pour at the correct temperature (see page 36), keeping some wax back for the second pour. Leave the candle to set for a short while. You may notice that as it sets a small dip or holes appear in the top of the candle.

5 If this occurs, reheat the saved wax and pour into any holes or dips (if necessary you can use a cocktail stick to enlarge small holes to ensure they are completely filled with new wax). Do not pour over the original height of the wax.

6 Leave the candle to set until completely cold. Remove the mould seal and the wick sustainer and the candle should easily come away from the mould. Leave to set and 'cure' for 48 hours before burning.

Using latex rubber or silicone moulds

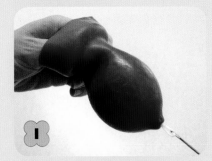

1 Take a primed wick and thread it through the end of a wicking needle. Pierce the bottom of the latex rubber or silicone mould, making sure that the hole is exactly in the centre, and pull the wick through the hole in the mould.

2 Place the mould in a special holder for rubber moulds.

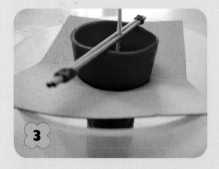

3 Alternatively, make a collar out of cardboard in which to insert the mould and place this over a glass or jug to hold it steady.

4 Now follow the instructions for pillar candles. Do not forget to treat the mould with a releasing agent if using beeswax. Once the candle is set, gently peel back the mould to reveal the candle. Leave to set and 'cure' for 48 hours before burning.

5 If you are making candles with fruit-shaped moulds you may like to paint the wicks with brown coloured wax to make the wicks look like the stems of the fruit.

Using items from around the home

You do not have to spend a lot of money on candle moulds. Providing that the wax is not poured at too high a temperature, plastic, metal, rubber or cardboard items from around the house can be used as moulds. Plastic food containers, drawer tidies and juice and milk cartons all make inexpensive candle moulds. However, if you want to make a pillar or moulded candle from a household item, make sure that the top of the mould is the same size or larger than the bottom otherwise you will not be able to unmould the candle.

Juice or milk carton

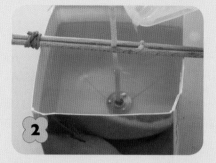

1 Use a large carton or cut a tall carton to size (if you don't have a small carton handy to use).

2 For a small (or cut-down) carton, glue a pre-tabbed waxed wick on the bottom of the container. If using a whole carton, suspend the wick over the candle with a wick sustainer. Now follow the instructions for making pillar candles (see pages 40–41).

Drawer tidy

Plastic drawer tidies make good rectangular moulds for candles. You will probably need to use several wicks for these. Use chopsticks or wooden skewers to hold your wicks in place.

Cardboard tubes

Potato chip/crisp tubes are perfect for making pillar candles (you will need to make sure that the bottom of the container is not completely flat and has a little lip so that you can seal your wick and the candle can still stand flat on the table).

1 Thoroughly clean the mould, and make a hole in the bottom with a metal skewer.

2 Thread the primed wick through the hole and seal with mould sealer, putty or Blu-Tack.

3 Secure the wick at the other end of the candle. To do this you can either use a wick sustainer or you can make a hole in the plastic lid of the container, cut the sides of the lid so that you can pour in the wax and thread the wick through the hole.

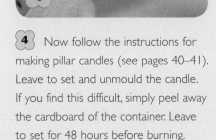

4 Now follow the instructions for making pillar candles (see pages 40–41). Leave to set and unmould the candle. If you find this difficult, simply peel away the cardboard of the container. Leave to set for 48 hours before burning.

Votive candles

These candles are somewhere in between a pillar and a container candle. They are often sold on their own without a container, but should always be burned in one. Votive candles are generally around 2in (5cm) high and 1¾in (4.5cm) in diameter. Votives are slightly tapered, with the bottom diameter being slightly smaller than the top. They are made with soya pillar wax or beeswax and will typically burn for about 10–15 hours. Votive candles are made in special metal 'votive' moulds (you can also sometimes find several votive moulds on one polycarbonate sheet).

Making the candle

1 Melt, colour and fragrance the soya pillar wax or beeswax at the correct temperature (see page 36) and pour into the mould without a wick. Leave the wax to set for just a minute or two. As soon as the wax around the sides of the mould starts to set (the wax will begin to look pale), place a pre-tabbed waxed wick into the wax. The setting wax at the bottom of the mould should hold the tab in place. Use a wick sustainer if necessary to hold the wick in place.

2 If you are making a layered candle (see page 59), leave the wax to set until the wax is firm enough to hold the weight of the next layer of wax, but still warm, to allow the next layer to adhere to it. Save some wax in case you need to do a second pour to fill any dips or holes in the top of the candle.

3 Remove the candle when ready. Unlike other moulded candles where the top of the candle is actually the bottom, remember that for a votive candle the top of the mould will be the actual top of the candle.

Votive wick pins

You can also purchase votive wick pins. These are round metal discs with a metal rod attached. The votive pin is placed inside the votive mould and the wax is poured around the pin. When unmoulded a hole is left in the candle through which you can slot your pre-tabbed waxed wick.

Container candles

To make container candles, both your room and the containers should be at approximately 70°F (21°C); you can gently heat the containers in the oven or heat them with a hairdryer if they are really cold. The temperature difference between the wax and the container should be as little as possible so that the wax adheres well to the sides of the container. If the temperature difference is too great, you may experience 'wet spots' or frosting on the sides of glass containers where small sections of the wax have visibly pulled away from the edge of the container. This creates no problem in the quality of your candle; it is just less aesthetically pleasing.

1 Take a pre-tabbed, waxed/primed wick and dab a piece of wax glue, a glue dot, or hot glue from a gun onto the base of the metal tab and affix to the bottom of the container.

2 Make sure that you place the wick exactly in the centre of the container otherwise the candle will burn unevenly.

3 If the container is a little deep for your hand to fully reach in to secure the wick tab, use a chopstick or end of a wooden spoon to press it in place.

5 Heat the wax to 155°F (68°C) or 190°F (87°C) if using powder dye. Colour and scent the wax and pour at between 125°F (51°C) and 155°F (68°C); see pages 37–39. Leave to set and 'cure' for 48 hours before burning.

4 Make sure that you wick the candle appropriately for your type of container. Refer to the section 'Selecting a wick', on pages 30–33, for advice.

Multi-wicked container candles

For larger container candles or pillar candles that are larger than 4in (10cm) in diameter, you will need to use more than one wick (see the wick guide on page 32). For a multi-wicked candle, try laying chopsticks or wooden skewers across the top of the mould to help the wicks stay in position.

Wooden wicks

Wooden wicks are wicked in exactly the same way as any other wick. They usually come with tabs (small metal discs), which you can glue to the bottom of your container as you would for a normal tabbed wick but the wick can also be suspended.

1 Suspend the wick over the container and hold it in the right position with wick sustainers. You could also use two wooden sticks held together with elastic bands.

2 When the candle is set, trim the wooden wick to approximately ¼in (0.5cm) with a pair of wood wick trimmers, (these are inexpensive and sold by candlemaking suppliers).

Tea lights

These are effectively mini container candles. They are made with soya container wax and contained in little round metal or plastic cups that are usually around 1in (2.5cm) high.

Tea lights must always be placed in tea light holders and these cups should **never** be burned directly on a surface as this is a fire hazard.

1 Heat, colour, scent and pour the wax (follow the instructions on pages 35–39).

2 Leave the candles to set for a minute or two and then pop in pre-tabbed waxed tea light wicks. These should quickly become held in place by the setting wax. However, do not leave the candles to set for long. If a skin forms on the top of the wax you will disturb the smooth surface if you have to break any set wax to insert the wick.

Dipped candles and tapers

This is the oldest and most traditional way of making candles. A wick is repeatedly dipped into a tall dipping pot containing melted beeswax. Each time the wick is dipped into the melted beeswax it collects more wax. The candle gradually gets thicker until it reaches the required diameter. Dipped candles are usually used as dinner candles and placed in holders or candelabras. Use beeswax for these candles, as soya wax is not suitable.

You will need a candle dipping pot to make these candles. They are available from candlemaking suppliers. It may take a little patience to produce the candles, but they are fun to make and very rewarding.

1 Fill the dipping container with beeswax and melt in a pot of simmering water – ideally the water should reach approximately half way up the dipping pot if you can find a deep enough saucepan.

2 As the wax melts down you may want to add more wax to fill up the container. Add the colour (and candle fragrance if you are using scent). However, these are perhaps best unfragranced as they are more commonly used as dinner candles.

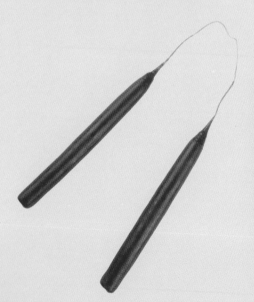

3 Double a length of wick in half and cut both ends so they are longer than the dipping pot. When the temperature reaches approx. 165°F (73°C) hold the wick in the middle and dip the full length of both wicks into the melted wax until the ends just touch the bottom of the pot. The dip should be a slow, steady movement.

4 Leave the wicks hanging over a nail or dipping arm (available from suppliers) for 2–3 minutes between each dip making sure that the candles do not touch each other. Keep dipping in this way and the wax will gradually build on each candle. You may need to dip 20–40 times to achieve the desired width. During this time the wax in your pot will start to cool so make sure that you maintain the temperature of 165°F (73°C). You will also need to top up the wax in your dipping pot as the wax gets used up in making the candles. When you have finished dipping you can trim the ends of the candles with a knife if desired. Leave for 24 hours before burning.

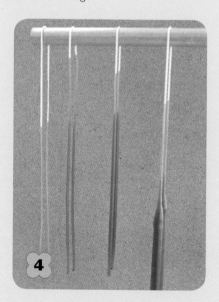

Twisted dipped candles

1 When you have finished the last dip of the candle, leave it to set for a little while. When set, but still warm and pliable, flatten the candle with a rolling pin to a thickness of about ¼in (0.5cm). Leave the bottom 1in (2.5cm) of the candle unflattened so that it will fit into a candle holder.

2 Working quickly so that the wax does not become too hard, hold the candle at the wick end and gently twist the wax with your other hand. You can trim the ends of the candles with a knife if desired. Leave to set for 24 hours before burning.

Rolled beeswax candles

Rolled candles are made from pliable ready-made sheets of honeycombed beeswax, which are available as natural or in different colours. These are probably the easiest candles to make as this does not involve heating the wax. The wax is simply rolled around a wick.

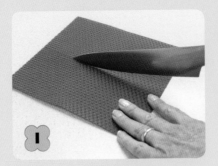

1 With a kitchen knife, cut a 3¾in x 8in (10cm x 20cm) piece of beeswax sheet. The beeswax sheet must be at room temperature so that it is pliable. If it is cold, you can gently heat it with a hairdryer or place it near a radiator or other warm place.

2 Choose a square-braided wick one size smaller than the diameter of your finished candle. Cut the wick (which does not have to be primed) ½in (1cm) longer than the length of the sheet (or length of candle). Place the wick ¼in (0.5cm) from edge of the wax.

Other ideas

If you cut the sheet at an angle along the wick side edge of the beeswax, this will result in a tapered top. Use several sheets of beeswax, or a larger sheet, to make thicker or longer candles. Alternatively, use a few differently coloured sheets of beeswax rolled together for a multicoloured effect.

3 Gently turn up the edges of the beeswax and fold it over the wick. Continue rolling the beeswax, making sure that the ends of the candle are square and even.

4 When you get to the end of the beeswax, gently press the edge of the wax with your fingers, or fix with wax glue.

Sand candles

1 Put some sand in a bowl or bucket and dampen with water. Press a jar or other simple shape into the sand to make an impression.

2 Remove the jar or shape to reveal a void in the sand.

3 Place a primed wick in the void and hold in place with a wick sustainer. Melt, colour and fragrance your soya pillar wax or beeswax at the correct temperature and pour into your mould (see pages 35–39).

4 When set, simply lift the candle out of the sand and brush off the excess sand. Leave to set and 'cure' for 48 hours before burning.

Whipped wax (and mini snowballs)

To make whipped wax for pillar candles, first make a base candle for decorating. Whipped wax has the texture and appearance of whipped cream or frosty snow and is particularly suited to food and snowy themes (make sure that food-type candles are labelled 'do not eat' and keep them well away from children).

1 Make the candle base ready for decorating with whipped wax.

2 Melt some pillar wax and leave it to cool. When it starts to pale up, whip it with a fork as if you are whipping cream.

3 As soon as the wax resembles whipped cream and is solid enough to hold its form, quickly apply it to the base candle.

4 If you work too slowly the wax will solidify and become crumbly. If this happens, simply reheat and start again.

5 If you have any whipped wax left over, take some in your hands and roll into a ball. The ball should be larger than 2½in (6.5cm) in diameter. Quickly make a hole with a skewer all the way through the wax for the wick and leave to set. When the candle is set thread a pre-tabbed waxed wick through the hole in the ball and trim the top to ¼in (0.5cm).

Decorating whipped wax

Decorative items such as embeds made from pillar wax or items made from beeswax sheets such as rolled 'cherries' or 'flakes' can be gently pressed into the whipped wax while it is soft – but you will need to be fast as it will set quickly.

1 Tear a small area from the beeswax sheet.

2 Roll into a ball in your fingers.

3 Push the decoration into the whipped wax.

Floating candles

As long as a candle is wider than it is tall it should float in water. Floating candles are made from soya pillar blend wax or beeswax.

1 Heat, scent and colour the candles. If you are feeling creative you can make differently coloured candles. With a spoon, scoop up a little wax of each colour and dribble into the next mould to achieve a multicoloured effect. Special floating candle moulds can be purchased or you can use mini muffin trays or cookie cutter shapes.

2 Wait for the wax to set slightly as you would for votive candles and pop in a pre-tabbed waxed wick. Make sure that the wick is primed so that it does not absorb water. If your candles are small you can use votive or tea light wicks.

Cookie cutter candles

Wax shapes can be cut out using cookie cutters and stacked to make a pillar candle. Melt, scent and colour the soya pillar or beeswax to the required temperature (see pages 35–39) and pour into a lightly greased or foil-lined baking tray.

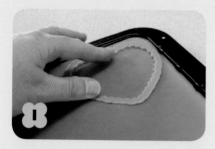

1 Make sure that the depth of wax is not greater than the depth of the cutter. Leave to set so that the wax is solid but still warm and pliable. If it is too hard, the shapes will crack (if this does happen simply melt all of the wax and start again).

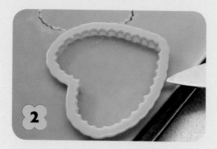

2 Gently press the cookie cutter into the wax and lift the cutter away leaving an imprint in the wax. Keep cutting shapes until the whole of the sheet is full. If you do not have a cookie cutter you could simply divide the baking tray into squares, rectangles or triangles with a knife.

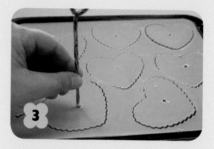

3 Make holes in the centre of the shapes with a skewer. Work quickly so that the wax does not set.

4 Turn the baking tray upside down and release the wax sheet.

5 Carefully press out each shape.

6 Take a primed wick with a metal tab on the end and thread this through the hole of each shape until you have built up a pillar of stacked shapes.

Aroma melts/wax tarts and wax embeds

These are fragranced wax shapes without wicks made from soya pillar blend wax and placed in special oil or tart burners, which are heated by a tea light underneath. The tea light melts the wax filling the little bowl in the tart burner and scenting the room.

Heat, scent and colour the wax in the usual way. Pour the wax into ice cube moulds, mini silicone or polycarbonate tart moulds and leave to set. Place the shape in an oil or tart burner and light a tea light underneath to heat the wax. To double your scent, you could make your own tea lights using the same fragrance as the aroma melts.

These useful wax shapes can also be embedded in wax for decorative effects in container candles.

Use soya pillar wax to make these embeds for containers, otherwise they will not unmould.

Layered and angled candles

To make layered candles, melt two or three differently coloured batches of wax and scent each one. If you are making a floating, votive, pillar/moulded candle, use soya pillar or beeswax. For making layered container candles in jars, use soya container wax.

1 Wick your candle and pour the first layer of wax. The layering method is the same for all types of wax. If you are making an angled candle, tip the container to one side and prop it up with a kitchen towel or piece of cardboard. Leave the wax to set until it is firm enough to hold the weight of the next layer, but still warm so that the next layer will adhere to it. While you are waiting for the wax to set, heat your second batch of coloured wax.

2 Pour the next layer. If you are making an angled candle, tilt the candle in another direction and for the final layer, keep the container upright so that you have a flat top to the candle.

3 Make sure that the pouring wax is not too hot otherwise it will start to melt the previous layer. You may wish to purposefully do this so that the two layers merge and marble together, you can also marble them further with a cocktail stick or skewer.

Using old scraps of wax

Old scraps of wax or candles can be re-melted down to make new ones. Keep a plastic bag for each different type of wax, i.e. pillar wax, container wax, beeswax so that you only use the appropriate wax for the type of candle. Old pieces of container wax cannot be used in pillar candles, etc.

1 To make a pillar candle out of old coloured wax chips, place them in a mould and fill the rest of the mould with melted uncoloured, unscented wax.

2 Melt the soya pillar wax or beeswax and pour at the correct temperature (see page 36). Keep some wax back for your second pour (refer to making pillar candles on pages 40–41 for full instructions).

Decorating candles

You can, of course, leave your candles plain and simple, but it can sometimes be fun to decorate the outside of them for an extra special effect. Over the next few pages, we show you ways of decorating and enhancing the exterior of your candle with cut-out wax shapes and transfers, by giving it a shimmering effect with overdips and pearlizers or by stencilling a pattern.

Appliqué

1 Appliqué wax sheets are available in a multitude of colours and metallics from which you can cut your own decorative shapes using little sugarcraft cutters to then affix to your candle.

2 To cut out a shape, gently press a small cutter into the wax as if you are cutting a little cookie. You can also purchase ready-cut appliqué wax shapes or you can cut shapes from the appliqué wax with a knife. Warm the shape with your hands and press directly onto the candle. Alternatively, place a dab of wax glue on the shape and affix to your candle.

Candle transfers

Some candle suppliers sell picture transfers, or metallic transfer sheets to apply to candles. These can be tricky to work with but are effective if you have the patience. Place the transfer on the candle and rub the back to transfer the design. Eventually the transfer should adhere to the candle, but you may have to help it along by gently peeling it off with your fingers. Try a sample first to make sure that it will transfer to your type or blend of wax before purchasing lots of them.

Beeswax sheets

Coloured sheets of honeycomb beeswax are available in lots of colours and can be used in a similar way to appliqué wax. Cut your desired shape and affix to your candle with wax glue. Pieces of beeswax sheet can also be rolled into tubes or moulded with the fingers to create shapes – make sure that the beeswax is at room temperature so that it is pliable.

Pearlizing lacquer/metallic overdips

This is often available in pearl, silver and gold and is useful for overpouring and overdipping candles without edges, such as eggs, spheres and cones. They are a great way of adding a bit of shimmer and glamour to your candles. They are particularly effective for wedding, festive and special-occasion candles.

Bronzing powder

This powder is usually available in silver, gold and bronze for giving your candle a metallic sheen. It is a very fine powder and gets absolutely everywhere so be very careful when using this before bronzing your entire kitchen or workshop.

1 Place your candle and the bronzing powder on a sheet of paper or newspaper and carefully brush on the powder.

2 Fix it in place by heating with a hairdryer.

Other ideas for decorating candles

Overdipping

Another way of giving your candle a colourful or shimmering finish is to overdip it. Cut the wick a little longer than normal, melt the wax and add either a contrasting colour or some metallic overdipping paste. Holding the candle by the wick, either half dip into the contrasting colour (for a two-tone effect) or dip the whole candle to entirely coat it with colour.

Candle glitter

Add a little sparkle to your candle with some candle glitter. There are varying types available to buy, so follow your supplier's instructions.

Candle-decorating pens

These candle pens come in a vast range of colours and metallics. They can be used to write or draw a unique design directly onto the candle.

Stencilling or stamping

Liven up a plain candle by stencilling or stamping a design onto it. Stamps and stencils can be purchased from craft shops or you can make your own stencil cut out from paper. Pieces of old lace or paper doilies can create pretty patterns on wedding candles, particularly when used with metallic paints.

Fix the stencil to the candle and lightly spray a non-toxic paint over it. If using a sponge, dip it in a little acrylic paint and press over the stencil. Alternatively, paint a stamp with acrylic paint (practice on paper first) and roll from side to side on the candle (make sure that you do not spray your paint near a naked flame or burning candle).

You can also stick non-flammable items such as metallic foil, gems, beads and shells to the outside of your candle. Fix them on by painting some melted wax glue to the back of the object.

A candle decorated with glitter.

A tube of candle glitter.

Candle-decorating pens.

Test burning and safety

Test burning a candle

If you are selling, or giving your candle away as a present, you must always test burn your candle first. Light the candle, burn for the various burn periods on the test-burning sheet (see page 67) and record your findings. If you are testing lots of candles, label each one with a batch number and record this number on the sheet.

Don't forget to label your candles if test burning in a batch.

Test different wicks

Leave your candle to settle or 'cure' for at least 48 hours. To save making lots of the same candle to test several different wicks, make a candle without a wick. Take a wicking needle, skewer or drill bit about the same diameter as the wick and make a hole where the wick should be. Place a primed wick in the hole, light the candle and record the burn qualities. If you need to try a different-sized wick, take out the old wick while the wax is still melted, leave to set again, make another hole and place in the new wick.

However, if you wish to compare, for example, three candles with different wicks all burning alongside each other, it is perhaps best to make three separate candles with three wicks.

Test burning is the best way find the wick most suited to your candle.

How to test burn a container candle

1 Trim the wick to ¼in (0.5cm).

2 Measure the diameter of the candle in inches – i.e. 2in.

3 Burn the candle for the same number of hours i.e. 2 hours.

4 In this amount of time, you should achieve a burn pool depth (depth of melted wax) of ¼ – ½in (0.5–1cm).

5 The wax should be completely melted from side to side.

6 If you have a larger burn pool, your candle smokes, or your wick mushrooms badly (has an excessive build up of carbon), you may need a smaller wick, a different fragrance or less fragrance.

7 If you do not achieve the full ¼in (0.5cm) burn pool in the timescale calculated, try a larger wick.

Calculating the burn time of your candle

1 Weigh your candle (if using a container, subtract weight of the empty container from your total weight). You only want the weight of the wax (start weight)	e.g. 7oz (200g)
2 Burn the candle for 3 hours (test-burn hours)	
3 Weigh your candle again (end weight)	e.g. 6.3oz (180g)
4 Subtract the end weight from the start weight	e.g. 7oz (200g) − 6.3oz (180g) = 0.7oz (20g)
5 Divide the lost wax weight between the number of test-burn hours	e.g. 0.7oz (20g) ÷ 3 (hours) = 0.23oz (6.66g)
Summary Original candle weight (start weight) Minus the weight after 3 test-burn hours = Lost wax during burning Divide by number of test-burn hours **This is your burn rate per hour**	7oz (200g) 6.3oz (180g) 0.7oz (20g) ÷ 3 (hours) = 0.23oz (6.66g)
Original candle weight (start weight) Divide by hourly burn rate **This is your total burn rate**	7oz (200g) ÷ 0.23oz (6.66g) = 30 hours

Your candle will therefore burn 0.23oz (6.66g) of wax per hour. If your original candle weight was 7oz (200g), this means that your candle will burn for approxiamately 30 hours.

Blank test-burning sheet

Batch no. (write this number on a sticker and affix to your candle)	
Date	
Start time of test burn	
End time of test burn	
Type of wax	
Type, size and number of wicks	
Type of mould/container used	
Size/diameter of candle/mould	
Name and supplier of fragrance	
Amount of fragrance/essential oil	
Colour	
Room temperature °F (°C)	
Temperature of containers if heated	
Wax pouring temperature	
Curing time	
Appearance – wet spots, frosting, blooming	

Results – burn quality

Time	Scent throw (hot/cold)*	Burn-pool size	Flame size	Sooting/other
30 minutes				
1 hour				
2 hours				
3 hours				
4 hours				

* Hot scent throw is how strong the fragrance smells when the candle is lit. Cold scent throw is how strong the fragrance smells when the candle is unlit and cold.

Fire precautions

Keep a tub of bicarbonate of soda (baking soda) next to your melting pot as it is good for smothering flames. It will not always be apparent when your wax is about to combust so you must always keep checking the temperature.

Cleaning up spilt wax

If you spill soya wax on the floor or kitchen surface, leave it to set and simply scrape it up. Clean any excess with hot soapy water. If you spill soya wax on your clothing or carpet, wash it with hot soapy water.

If you spill beeswax on a carpet or clothing, put some absorbent paper towels on top of the spillage and place a warm iron on top of the paper. This will melt the wax and the paper will absorb some of the melted wax. You will need to repeat this process and keep replacing the absorbent paper as the wax gets absorbed. Alternatively you could put the item in the freezer or rub with an ice cube and remove some of the solidified wax this way. If all else fails take your item of clothing to the dry cleaners.

In the event of a fire:

- **Leave the pan where it is – do not pick it up or move it.**

- **Turn off the electric power or heat source.**

- **DO NOT USE WATER – wax is like oil so never use water to extinguish a wax fire; instead smother the flames.**

- **Smother the flames with bicarbonate of soda, fire blanket, fire extinguisher, damp cloth, metal lid or metal baking tray.**

- **Call the fire brigade.**

If you burn your skin with hot wax:

- **Immediately immerse your skin in cool water.**

- **For mild burns treat with aloe vera or visit your pharmacy for over-the-counter burn treatments.**

- **If the burn badly blisters, turn off your electric heat supply (don't rush off and forget to turn off your melting pot), and then go to the nearest clinic, hospital or burns unit.**

Labelling your candles

If you want to give your candle as a present or sell to the public, you **must** label your candles with fire safety precautions. Some, or all of the information below should be added to your candle label depending on your type of candle. Picture warnings can also be included. You may also be required to state burn times or weight of the candle so contact your local or national trading standards department or candle guild for full advice on selling your candles.

Safety warnings:

• **Never leave a burning candle unattended.**

• **Burn away from combustibles.**

• **Keep away from children and pets.**

• **Burn candles away from draughts.**

• **Trim wick to ¼in (0.5cm) before each burn and remove carbon or match debris from candle.**

• **On first lighting your candle, burn to a full burn pool to achieve even burning thereafter and to avoid a tunnelling effect on subsequent burns.**

• **Do not burn for more than 4 hours at a time.**

• **Do not burn the last ½in (1cm) of container candles to avoid excess heating of the container.**

• **Place on a heat-resistant surface.**

• **Tea lights should always be placed in an appropriate tea light holder and should never placed directly on to a surface.**

Troubleshooting

Here are some of the common problems and solutions that may occur when you are making your candles:

Problem	Solutions
The flame is large and smoking	Trim your wick to ¼in (0.5cm) or use a smaller wick.
Mushrooming: carbon or soot build-up on wick	Wick is too large; try a different size or type of wick. Fragrance or essential oil is incompatible or there is too much fragrance or essential oil.
The flame is small and the wick is drowning or extinguished in wax	Your wick is too small and cannot consume all of the melted wax. Change to a larger wick.
Wax is sweating on top of my soya candle	Too much fragrance or essential oil or the fragrance is incompatible with your wax. Change or cut down on either or both.
Glass container candle appears to have wet spots or areas of different-coloured soya wax on the sides of the container	The difference between the temperature of your containers and the wax may have been too great and the wax has pulled away from your container in parts and not adhered to the sides. Heat your containers in an oven or with a hairdryer if they are too cold – they should be room temperature. The candles have cooled too quickly. Your room temperature should be around 70°F (21°C). Candles have been stored at too low a temperature, they should be stored at around 70°F (21°C).

Problem	Solutions
A chalky white substance has appeared on the top of my soya candle	This is known as 'frosting' or 'bloom' and is a change in the crystal structure of the wax similar to the bloom that can appear on chocolates. This can result if: • The pouring temperature was too high. • Candles were cooled too quickly. • Storage of candles was too cold (this will disappear in a few days if the candles are moved to a storage area of 70°F/21°C). • The containers were too close together while cooling. They need to be at least ½in (1cm) apart so that the air can circulate. The containers should remain open for 24 hours while setting. Heat the surface with a hairdryer or heat gun to remove frosting.
Holes or craters have appeared in the top of my soya container candle	Try pouring your wax at a lower temperature. Reduce the temperature in 10°F (or 6°C) increments and record your findings. It may also be due to trapped air. Make sure you pour your wax slowly to reduce air bubbles. Heat the surface with a hairdryer or heat gun to even out any holes, this will briefly melt the wax and smooth the surface again. When the trapped air rises to the surface, pop it with a pin.
Candle burns a tunnel of wax downwards in my container	The wick is too small. You didn't burn the candle for long enough on the first burn to achieve a full burn pool – this changes the structure of the wax so that each burn pool thereafter continues to produce a full burn pool.

Basic ingredients

Essential oils

What are essential oils?

Essential oils are used in the practice of aromatherapy to help ease a multitude of complaints and conditions while at the same time affecting moods and wellbeing. Aromatherapy is the term for a non-medical complementary holistic treatment of caring for the body via inhalation or topical application of aromatic plant oils. They have been used for centuries for their antiseptic, antiviral, antifungal and antibacterial properties in the control of infections.

Essential oils are the highly fragrant natural volatile oils of plants, leaves, fruit, seeds, roots, wood, resin, gum, grasses and flowers, which are produced by the plant to either protect itself against bacteria or fungus, or to encourage fertilization. They are not 'oils' as such; they are more like water in consistency and are the spirit, personality or essence of an aromatic plant.

Safety

Most essential oils should be avoided by young children and the recipes in this book that contain essential oils are not intended for use by children under the age of seven. Recipes can always be adapted by using candle fragrance oil instead.

Advice from a qualified practitioner or medical adviser should be sought if you: have a known medical condition such as high blood pressure or epilepsy, are receiving any psychiatric or medical treatment, taking medication, are pregnant or breast-feeding.

Storage

Store essential oils in dark-coloured glass jars or bottles in a cool environment. Essential oils may damage clothing and wooden surfaces, so cover up before using them.

Directory of essential oils

There are too many essential oils to list in this section and some are prohibitively expensive to use in candles. Some of the known therapeutic properties of each oil that may benefit you when inhaling the scent from an aromatherapy candle are listed. The letter after the name of each oil denotes whether it is a top **(T)**, middle **(M)** or base note **(B)**. **(T, M)** indicates a top to middle note that may be used as either. The perfume and fragrance section (see pages 81–85) contains information on how to blend your own aromatherapy candle scents using these oils.

Basil (T)

Ocimum basilicum

Fragrance: light, fresh, green, sweet, with a balsamic undertone.

Known uses: nervous system, tension, memory, headache, migraine, respiratory complaints, colds, concentration, fatigue.

Blends with: rose geranium, cedarwood, ginger, grapefruit, lavender, lemon, sweet orange, lemongrass and lime.

Camphor (white) (T)

Cinnamomum camphora

Fragrance: pungent, sharp, clear, fresh.

Known uses: lungs, bronchitis, coughs, colds, fever, flu, infectious diseases, convalescence, nervous depression.

Blends with: basil, chamomile and lavender.

Cedarwood (B)

Cedrus atlantica or *Juniperus virginiana*

Fragrance: clean, sharp, fresh, slightly sweet, woody, balsamic undertones.

Known uses: nervous system, stress, tension, respiratory problems, bronchitis, arthritis, rheumatism, insect repellent.

Blends with: cinnamon, frankincense, juniper, lavender, lemon, myrrh, sandalwood, vetiver and rosemary.

Chamomile (Roman) (M)

Anthemis nobilis

Fragrance: refreshing, sweet, herbaceous, fresh, apple-like.

Known uses: nervous complaints, stress, insomnia, headaches and migraines.

Blends with: clary sage, lavender, jasmine, grapefruit, lemon, ylang ylang, rose geranium.

Fresh basil

Dried chamomile

Cinnamon (M, B)

Cinnamomum zeylanicum

Fragrance: warm, spicy, powerful.

Known uses: bronchitis, colds, flu, circulation, weakness, depression.

Blends with: sweet orange, lemon, lime, patchouli, frankincense, lavender, rose geranium and rosemary.

Clary sage (T, M)

Salvia sclarea

Fragrance: sweet, nutty, rich, herbaceous.

Known uses: nervous tension, depression, stress, insomnia, aphrodisiac, menopause. Do not use during pregnancy or when drinking alcohol as it can make you drowsy.

Blends with: juniper, lavender, sandalwood, rose geranium, lemon, pine, frankincense and citrus oils.

Eucalyptus (T)

Eucalyptus globulus

Fragrance: strong medicinal, sharp, fresh, camphoraceous, with slight woody undertones.

Known uses: respiratory system, decongestant, colds, bronchitis, flu, hayfever.

Blends with: lavender, cedarwood, lemongrass, tea tree, lemon and pine.

Citronella (T)

Cymbopogon nardus

Fragrance: citrus, slightly sweet, fresh.

Known uses: insect repellent, nervous exhaustion, fatigue, colds, flu.

Blends with: cedarwood, lemon, sweet orange, grapefruit, pine, lavender and rose geranium.

Cinnamon sticks and powder

Clary sage

Eucalyptus

Frankincense (B)

Boswellia carterii

Fragrance: fresh top note with sweet, woody, resinous undertones.

Known uses: nervous tension, stress, respiratory conditions, coughs, asthma, bronchitis.

Blends with: petitgrain, pine, myrrh, sandalwood, cedarwood, vetiver, lavender, sweet orange and lemon.

Grapefruit (T)

Citrus grandis

Fragrance: fresh, green, zesty, sweet, citrus.

Known uses: nervous exhaustion, stress, lethargy, depression, insomnia, lymphatic system, hangovers, immune system, colds, flu.

Blends with: palmarosa, pine, frankincense, lavender, rose geranium, eucalyptus and pine.

Lemon (T)

Citrus medica limonum

Fragrance: fresh, sweet, green, citrus.

Known uses: antibacterial, fatigue, bronchitis, asthma, colds, flu, loss of voice, depression, stress, mental fatigue.

Blends with: lavender, rose geranium, sandalwood, eucalyptus, juniper and petitgrain.

Ginger (T, M)

Zingiber officinale

Fragrance: hot, dry, pungent and musty, with a lingering spicy sweetness.

Known uses: respiratory system, catarrh, colds, flu, fevers, immune system, nausea, aphrodisiac.

Blends with: all citrus and spicy oils and in particular, frankincense, rose geranium, sandalwood, ylang ylang, vetiver, juniper and cedarwood.

Lavender (T, M)

Lavandula angustifolia

Fragrance: fresh, light, soft, clean sweet floral.

Known uses: widely used for its numerous therapeutic benefits, including nervous problems, stress, insomnia, trauma, depression, respiratory system; also an insect repellent.

Blends with: all oils.

Ginger root

Grapefruit

Lavender

Lime (T)

Citrus aurantifolia

Fragrance: fresh, green, sharp, zesty citrus peel.

Known uses: antiviral, fatigue, depression, headaches, fevers, immune system, flu, bronchitis, sinusitis, travel sickness, digestion.

Blends with: juniper, petitgrain, lavender, clary sage, ylang ylang and citrus oils.

Mandarin (T)

Citrus nobilis

Fragrance: very sweet, rich, tangy, zesty-floral.

Known uses: nervous system, restlessness, tantrums, hyperactivity, stress, digestion.

Blends with: chamomile, lavender, frankincense, juniper, clary sage, lavender and petitgrain.

Myrrh (B)

Commiphora myrrha

Fragrance: dry, warm, musty, balsamic with rich, spicy sweet notes.

Known uses: antibacterial, antifungal, respiratory system, coughs, bronchitis, colds, reproductive system, anxiety, meditation.

Blends with: frankincense, lavender, cedarwood and sandalwood.

Orange (sweet) (T)

Citrus aurantium dulcis or sinensis

Fragrance: sweet, fresh, fruity smell.

Known uses: nervous system, depression, nervous tension headaches, anxiety, stress, digestive system, immune system, colds, flu.

Blends with: petitgrain, peppermint, ginger, frankincense, sandalwood, vetiver and lavender.

Palmarosa (M)

Cymbopogon martini

Fragrance: soft, sweet, rosy, floral with gentle notes of lemon.

Known uses: antiseptic, antiviral, convalescence, fatigue, nervousness, exhaustion, stress.

Blends with: rose geranium, sandalwood, sweet orange, grapefruit, chamomile, rosemary, lime and ylang ylang.

Patchouli (B)

Pogostemon cablin

Fragrance: aromatic, woody and musky with spicy, musty, earthy-sweet undertones.

Known uses: insect repellent, fungicide, depression, antiseptic, aphrodisiac.

Blends with: bergamot, rose geranium, clary sage, geranium, lavender, chamomile, cinnamon, cedarwood and myrrh.

Lime

Mandarin

Peppermint (T)

Mentha piperita

Fragrance: strong, fresh, minty, with sweet undertones.

Known uses: digestive system, nausea, headache, migraine, concentration, colds, coughs, insect repellent.

Blends with: Rosemary, ginger, eucalyptus, lavender, marjoram, lemon and rosemary.

Pine (T, M)

Pinus sylvestris

Fragrance: fresh, forest smell with sweet, balsamic tones.

Known uses: asthma, colds, flu, bronchitis, coughs, sinusitis, lethargy, hangover.

Blends with: cedarwood, lemon, eucalyptus, juniper, lavender and rosemary.

Rosemary (T, M)

Rosmarinus officinalis

Fragrance: strong, fresh, herbaceous, camphoraceous.

Known uses: sinusitis, memory, clear thinking, headaches, concentration, over-indulgence, colds, flu.

Blends with: Cedarwood, rose geranium, basil, lavender, lemongrass and peppermint.

Petitgrain (T)

Citrus aurantium

Fragrance: fresh, green, floral, with citrus and woody undertones.

Known uses: stress, panic, nervous exhaustion, depression, anger, digestion, convalescence, emotional conditions.

Blends with: juniper, clary sage, lavender, rosemary, sweet orange, lemon, palmarosa, sandalwood, chamomile, rose geranium and ylang ylang.

Rose geranium (T, M)

Pelargonium graveolens and *Pelargonium rosa*

Fragrance: fresh, crisp, rosy-sweet.

Known uses: nervous complaints, stress, mild depression, anxiety, tension, menopause.

Blends with: lime, cedarwood, clary sage, grapefruit, lavender, lemon, rosemary and orange.

Note

You can replace an expensive oil with one that has similar properties, or you can use a candle fragrance oil (but it will not have the therapeutic benefits). For instance, instead of rose oil, use palmarosa or rose geranium; petitgrain is a good replacement for neroli; use a jasmine candle fragrance instead of the real thing.

Rose geranium

Rosemary

Sandalwood (B)

Santalum album

Fragrance: soft, deep, rich, sweet, exotically woody.

Known uses: coughs, bronchitis, chest infections, asthma, insomnia, nervous tension, stress, exhaustion, insect repellent, meditation, aphrodisiac.

Blends with: palmarosa, rose geranium, vetiver, ylang ylang, lavender, cedarwood and myrrh.

Vanilla (B)

Vanilla planifolia

This is not actually an essential oil, but an extract from the vanilla bean.

Fragrance: sweet rich balsamic vanilla-like odour.

Known uses: stress, insomnia, anxiety, headache, depression.

Blends with: grapefruit, lemon, mandarin, orange, sandalwood and vetiver.

Ylang ylang (T, M)

Cananga odorata

Fragrance: intensely sweet, powerful, exotic, highly fragrant, floral scent with a creamy top note.

Known uses: stress, depression, exhaustion, tension, shock, fear, panic, anxiety, insomnia, rapid breathing, aphrodisiac.

Blends with: sandalwood, grapefruit, lavender, cedarwood, clary sage, lemon and vetiver.

Tea Tree (M)

Melaleuca alternifolia

Fragrance: fresh, strong, spicy, pungent camphoraceous smell.

Known uses: Immune system, shock, colds, flu, sinusitis, bronchitis, antiviral, antibacterial, antifungal.

Blends with: clove, lavender, eucalyptus, rosemary, pine, lemon and thyme.

Vetiver (B)

Vetiveria zizanoides

Fragrance: heavy, sweet, earthy, warm, smoky, with woody, musty undertones.

Known uses: nervous system, stress, exhaustion, depression, insomnia, hormone imbalance.

Blends with: clary sage, lavender, rose geranium, sandalwood, patchouli and ylang ylang.

Vanilla pods

Perfume and fragrance

Our sense of smell

Odours are important because they can alert us to danger such as a fire or rancid food that is poisonous. Young mammals need their olfactory sense (smell) to detect their mother's milk for feeding. Some scientists believe that we may unknowingly select our mate via aromatic chemicals called pheromones. However, the human sense of smell has been lost somewhat during evolution. We no longer need to negotiate our environment by our sense of smell as other animals do, or smell the scent of our enemy.

Humans can remember up to 10,000 different odours. As we breathe in odorous molecules, they travel up the nose, past olfactory receptor cells and send electrical signals to the brain. This can instantly trigger distinctive associations from the past such as a childhood trip, a place, or other pleasant or unpleasant memories.

What is perfume?

The word perfume (parfum) stems from the Latin *per* meaning through, and *fumum* meaning smoke – 'through smoke'. This is an indication of how early perfumes were produced; they were made by burning materials such as wood, gums and resins to give a fragrant smoke (incense). This is still used in places of worship and for meditation today.

Perfumiers choose from thousands of natural essential oils and synthetic 'aroma chemicals' for their formulations. The process of perfume blending is a highly skilful and complicated one, taking years of experience and training and requiring a particular 'nose' for the job. Just one drop of an ingredient can make the difference between an ordinary and an outstanding perfume. However, expensive essential oils are now only used in small amounts just to enhance a perfume, so most perfumes or fragrances will have little, or no therapeutic effects.

Top, middle and base notes

Fragrant ingredients used to create perfumes are categorized by their 'notes'. A fragrance, or perfume, is made up of top, middle and base notes.

Top notes are small molecules and are the first notes that hit you on smelling a fragrance thereby creating the first impression. Assertive, fresh, sharp and bright, they are initially powerful and intense, stimulating the senses, but they are the first notes to disappear.

Next the **middle notes** start to come through. These are generally warm, soft and mellow oils that provide the heart and body of a fragrance, rounding it off, and giving it complexity. They pave the way for the next level of oils to emerge. These can be unpleasant on their own, but with the partnership of the middle notes give support and durability.

The **base notes**, or 'theme', of the fragrance are usually heavy, exotic, sensual and warm and are generally woody or resinous materials. These aromas will be the last scents to be detected, lingering the longest and 'fixing' the whole blend, holding the top and middle notes from evaporating too quickly.

Creating your own blends

The following instructions are to enable you to blend your own scent for use in candles. They are **not** 'perfumes' or 'Eau de Toilettes' for spraying on the body, and as with all essential oils should **never** be used neat on the body. Blending your own essential oils is easy to do and you need only use a few ingredients if you wish.

Get to know your scents

Become familiar with your essential oils, making notes of your findings. If you create a stunning fragrance you will want to make sure that you know exactly how it was formulated.

When smelling an essential oil, do not put your nose directly over the top of the oil and vigorously sniff, otherwise you will get the full blast of the molecules up your nose and the scent will remain in the nostrils for some time, making it very difficult for you to smell any more odours for a while.

Prepare some strips of paper (such as coffee filter bags) which you can use to blot some of the oil and waft the scented paper gently to and fro under your nose. Let the fragrance lift upwards, and breathe in slowly. You will usually only be able to sample around six scents at a time before you get nose fatigue.

To fully appreciate a fragrance you should smell the scent from your paper testing strips as they can smell quite different once they are out of the bottle. If you have to smell a scent directly from the bottle, note that you will not be getting the full aroma – try smelling the cap instead of the bottle.

If your nose becomes overpowered, go outside in the fresh air to clear your nasal passages, or wave your hand over your nose to bring clear air into your nostrils. If you have a cold, or if you smoke, this will impair your sense of smell. It is important to take breaks every so often as essential oils are highly concentrated and sampling them for long periods at a time may cause headaches or nausea.

Blending your perfume

Firstly decide on a theme for your therapeutic blend. Keep things simple to start with; try not to overcomplicate your blend using a multitude of oils to create a one-stop cure-all recipe.

Once you have chosen your theme, use the essential oils directory on pages 75–80 as a guide. Beside each oil we have indicated the notes i.e. T (top), M (middle) or B (base). These are guides only as oils vary from batch to batch depending on how they have been extracted, where they come from and the type of species, therefore some will cross over the 'note' boundaries. Select a good balance of top, middle and base notes.

Start with the base oils, then the middle and finally the top notes. Some people start from the top and work down (it is a personal choice). Formulate your own personal blend using scents that are applicable to your theme and that complement each other.

First write down the oils and the amounts you think you will use. Following the chart below as an example, develop your perfume drop by drop. This way, if you do not like the end result, you can easily replicate your blend, and leave out or add ingredients as desired.

Perfume blending chart (with example)

Name of blend Eau de Cologne	No. of drops/parts	No. of drops/parts	No. of drops/parts	No. of drops/parts
Oil/fragrance	1st formula	2nd formula	3rd formula	4th formula
Bergamot	32			
Petitgrain	30			
Lemon	30			
Neroli	10			
Lavender	10			
Orange	2			
Total number of drops	114			

Using a pipette, drop the first essential oil from your written formula into a clean bottle. Make sure that the drop doesn't hit the sides of the glass bottle as the oil will cling to the sides for some time and you will not get the true amounts of oil in the bottom of your bottle.

Use a different pipette for each essential oil so that you do not contaminate individual oils. You can purchase caps with built-in droppers for essential oil bottles, which are perfect for this purpose.

Make sure that all of your drops are the same size – a drop from a pipette held sideways will create a much larger drop than one dropped from holding the pipette straight above the bottle.

Once you have developed your new fragrance, leave it if possible for a few days as the oils will react and blend with each other over this time.

Important note

Do not forget to label and date your blend and keep well away from children and pets. Store in a cool, dark place in a coloured glass bottle.

After several days, dip your testing strip into your blend and sample the fragrance, waving it gently under your nostrils. Leave the testing strip for a few hours, come back and sample again. If you are happy with the fragrance, make a note of it.

Approximate measures:

1ml = 20 drops
1 tsp (5ml) = 100 drops
1 fluid oz = 5 tsp (25ml)

Blending a perfume

1 Blend the essential oils into a clean bottle, using its built-in dropper cap.

2 Dip your testing strip into the blend to soak up some of the fragrance for sampling.

3 Wave the testing strip gently underneath your nose and then sample again after a few hours.

Combinations of candle fragrances

You will not be able to create your own 'fragrance oil' using essential oils as these are professionally made with aroma chemicals. If you want a chocolate, apple or sea breeze fragrance etc., you will have to purchase a ready-made candle fragrance oil (see suppliers list on pages 150–151).

Scent is usually the first sense to register on entering a home, so if you are selling your house, burning a vanilla, cinnamon, ginger or fudge scented candle in the kitchen will give the perception of a warm and cosy home. Fragrances such as floral, fresh and breezy scents can make your home feel larger as they give the perception of a clear outdoor space.

You can, however, blend candle fragrances together. For instance vanilla candle fragrance oil mixed with rose will give you 'baby powder', pineapple and coconut will create 'pina colada', peppermint and eucalyptus will give you 'fresh snow', etc. You may wish to start with just a few essential oils and fragrances. In the table below we have suggested the best ten fragrances to begin experimenting with. By selecting one from each line this will give you a good range to start blending your own bespoke candle fragrances. You can mix and match the essential oils with your candle fragrance oils; however, you will only know if the combination is right for your candle by test burning.

Ten of the best basic oils for blending

1	Lavender essential oil
2	Lemongrass, lemon or grapefruit essential oil
3	Rosemary or eucalyptus essential oil
4	Orange or mandarin essential oil
5	Rose candle fragrance oil or rose geranium essential oil
6	Vanilla essential oil, or vanilla candle fragrance oil
7	Pineapple or mango candle fragrance oil
8	Strawberry or passion fruit candle fragrance oil
9	Ocean or forest fresh candle fragrance oil
10	Cedarwood essential oil, aromatic wood or exotic spice candle fragrance oil

Colour therapy

Colour is light of different wavelengths and colour therapists believe that each colour has a specific vibration, which is absorbed through the eyes, skin and aura. These vibrations resonate with the different energy centres of the body and can unconsciously influence our physical, spiritual and emotional wellbeing. Colour is now being used in offices, hospitals, prisons and in marketing to create different moods.

Colour healing has been used since ancient times. In traditional Indian medicine it is believed that there are seven main spiralling energy centres of the body called chakras (pronounced sha-kra), the word meaning 'wheel'. Each chakra is associated with a particular colour and a different part of the body. A balance of each energy force is needed for good health and wellbeing.

When we are unwell or disturbed, our vibrations can be harmonized and equilibrium can be restored by using the appropriate colour. Focussing on the flame of a coloured candle is believed to amplify its healing colour vibrations, increasing the energy flow relating to the chakras.

To balance your energy system, choose a calm and peaceful place and sit comfortably. Using the chart on the next page, select a coloured candle that will resonate with the particular qualities of your chosen chakra. Light the candle, breathe deeply and use the candle as a tool to visualize the healing colour, to meditate, or to reinforce a specific goal.

Colour therapy can also be followed through into your home and office décor. Use the chart opposite to choose a colour and make a candle to place on your desk or dining table to help create different mood effects.

Just remember, however, that too much of one colour can produce an opposite effect. For instance, an excess of energy-giving red could create aggression and although blue can be calming, too much can be cold and unwelcoming.

Chakra and colour symbolism chart

Colour Chakra Related organ Endocrine gland	Therapeutic uses	Symbolism
Violet/purple **Crown chakra** **Brain** **Pineal gland**	Depression, mental disorders, Parkinson's, epilepsy, dementia, Alzheimer's, confusion, dizziness, headaches.	Spiritual or psychic awareness, self-knowledge, creativity, protection, leadership, concentration, rejuvenation.
Indigo **Brow chakra** **Eyes, lower head, sinuses** **Pituitary gland**	Migraine, tension headaches, depression, insomnia, visual sinus and ear problems.	Self-responsibility, higher intuition, faithful, integrity, calming, intelligence, trustworthiness.
Blue **Throat chakra** **Throat and lungs** **Thyroid gland**	Thyroid problems, anorexia, bronchitis, hearing, hormones, upper digestive tract, mouth ulcers, sore throat.	Communication, self-expression, truth, purpose, loyalty, trustworthy, calm, rest, serenity, peace, forgiveness, relaxation, cleansing, purification.
Green **Heart chakra** **Heart and breasts** **Thymus gland**	Heart disease, blood pressure, nervous system, immune system, anger, frustration.	Compassion, generosity, money, wealth, financial success, prosperity, luck, good harvest, fertility, shock, fatigue, stamina, cooperation, balance, harmony.
Yellow/gold **Solar plexus chakra** **Liver, spleen, stomach, small** **intestine, pancreas**	Nervous system, liver, digestion, diabetes, gall stones.	Self-worth, confidence, optimistic, attraction, charm, persuasion, cheerfulness, intellect, creativity, laughter, joy, fun.
Orange **Sacral chakra** **Uterus, large bowel, prostate** **Ovaries and testes**	Menstrual problems, fibroids, cysts, irritable bowel syndrome, testicular disease, urinary problems, lower back pain.	Self-respect, concentration, nerve stimulant, sociability, mind clearing, creativity, joyous, courage, independence, attraction, strong love, optimism, change.
Red **Base chakra** **Kidneys, bladder,** **vertebral column, hips, legs** **Adrenal gland**	Circulation, high blood pressure, diarrhoea, piles, constipation, colitis, kidney stones, impotence, fear, aches and pains, problems with hips, legs and feet.	Self-awareness, love, passion, sexuality, power, good health, vigour, excitement, fortune, energy, pioneering, assertiveness, strength and courage.

Although these colours are not chakra colours, they do have associated symbolisms

Colour	Therapeutic uses	Symbolism
White	Tonic, cleansing.	Truth, peace, purity, hope, precision, marriage, positivity, realization, spiritual strength, remembrance
Pink	Similar properties to red but more subtle. Aggression, violence disorders, insomnia, emotional pain, trauma.	Femininity, health, love, romance, calm, relaxation.

Recipes

Rummage around charity shops and flea markets to find pretty tea cups, tea pots or egg cups to use as unique and attractive containers. Light them at a garden tea party on a lovely summer's day.

Green tea

See pages 46–48 for instructions on making container candles

Ingredients

28oz (700ml or 805g) soya container wax
See the wick guide on page 32 to select a wick for testing
Meadow green colour
2 tablespoons (30ml) green tea candle fragrance oil

Containers

China tea cups

Quantity

This recipe will make approx. 4 candles

As children we have all loved playing in the sand! Sand candles are one of the easiest candles to make so use your imagination and be creative with your sand shapes.

Candle in the sand

See page 53 for instructions on making sand candles

Ingredients

8oz (200ml or 230g) soya pillar blend wax
See the wick guide on page 32 to select a wick for testing
1 tablespoon (15ml) lime flower and fig candle fragrance oil
Lime green and fudge colour

Mould

Make your impression/mould in the sand. Try using old food cartons, shells, jars or a glass bowl to make an impression.

Quantity

This recipe will make 1 candle

This candle is a tropical delight for your summer garden party. Let the deliciously fruity aroma waft in the breeze around your party table and bring the scent of the Caribbean to your guests on a hot sunny day.

Summer punch

See page 58 for instructions on making fruit embeds and pages 46–48 for making container candles

Ingredients

61oz (1500ml or 1.725kg) container wax
3½oz (100ml or 100g) soya pillar blend wax (fruit embeds)
See the wick guide on page 32 to select a wick for testing
3 tablespoons (45ml) tropical punch candle fragrance oil
Red and yellow (or peach) for container wax
Yellow and lime green for fruit embeds

Additional instructions

Make unfragranced fruit embeds and leave to set. Wick the candle and pour in the container wax. Leave until the surface of the wax has set slightly and will hold the fruit. Press the embeds into the wax. If the wax is too soft they will sink.

Container

Soup terrine (or thick-walled glass bowl)

Quantity

This recipe will make 1 large candle

Be your own fairy godmother by granting yourself three wishes.
Each colour has a different meaning. Refer to the colour therapy section
on pages 86–87 and see if your dreams really do come true.

Three wishes

See page 45 for instructions on making votive candles and page 59 on layering colours

Ingredients

14½oz (360ml or 415g) soya pillar wax
See the wick guide on page 32 to select a wick for testing
2 teaspoons (10ml) gardenia candle fragrance oil mixed with
2 teaspoons (10ml) daffodil candle fragrance oil
Pink, blue and yellow colours

Additional instructions

Wait until the first layer of wax has formed a skin thick enough to hold the next layer before pouring the second colour. Or, wait until a thin skin has formed and pour the next layer so that it mixes with the first layer for a marbled effect.

Moulds and containers

Votive moulds and glass holders

Quantity

This recipe will make 4 candles

You will probably not want to burn this mouth-watering candle as it looks just like the real thing, so place on a kitchen shelf or sideboard and have a calorie-free peek every now and then if you are watching your weight.

Sundae best

See page 55 for instructions on using beeswax sheets, page 59 on layering wax and page 54 for whipped wax

Ingredients

12oz (300ml or 345g) soya container wax
4oz (100ml or 115g) soya pillar blend wax
¼ sheet brown beeswax, small piece of red beeswax sheet
See the wick guide on page 32 to select a wick for testing
Pink and red (bottom layer), light pink (middle layer) colours
1 tablespoon (15ml) strawberry fragrance oil (container),
1 teaspoon (5ml) vanilla candle fragrance oil (topping)

Additional instructions

Roll the red beeswax into a ball and brown into cigar shape. Wick candle, pour the first layer, leave to set slightly then pour next layer. Leave to set until firm. Make whipped pillar wax and place on top. Press cherry and chocolate flake into the soft wax.

Containers

Glass sundae dish

Quantity

This recipe will make 1 candle

Aroma melts or wax tarts are a delightful way to fragrance a room. Place a melt in the top of an oil burner, light the tea light underneath and once the wax has melted the fragrance will flood the room with a sumptuous aroma.

Petits fours

See page 58 for instructions on making aroma melts

Ingredients

14oz (350ml or 400g) soya pillar blend wax
(7oz/175ml or 200g for each colour)
2 teaspoons (10ml) English rose candle fragrance oil
(use 1 teaspoon/5ml for each colour)
Girly pink and meadow green colour

Moulds

Silicone mini tart moulds and rose-shaped rubber moulds

Additional instructions

Melt the wax, add the pink colour to half of it and 1 teaspoon (5ml) fragrance. You may like to increase the amount of fragrance, but this will need testing. Do *not* increase the amount of fragrance much if you are using essential oils. Pour into the moulds, leave to cool until hard. Mix the green colour with the other half of the wax and the remaining 1 teaspoon (5ml) fragrance. Pour and leave to set.

Quantity

This recipe will make approx. 9 wax tarts and 9 aroma melts

Turn your bedroom into a 1930s glamour pad. Look for retro glass trinket sets in flea markets or on auction sites and fill with feminine, floral-scented wax. Then light a candle and pad around in your fluffy-heeled slippers.

Boudoir chic

See pages 46–48 for instructions on making container candles

Ingredients

6oz (150ml or 170g) container soya wax
See the wick guide on page 32 to select a wick for testing
1 teaspoon (5ml) rose candle fragrance oil
1 teaspoon (5ml) non-discolouring vanilla candle fragrance oil
Light pink colour

Containers

Pretty glass dishes

Quantity

This recipe will make approx. 3 small candles

It is late in the evening and you still have a pile of work to get through.
Light this candle to flood your office with this revitalizing aromatherapy blend,
which will awaken your senses and clear your head.

The midnight oil

*See pages 40–41 for instructions on making pillar candles and
page 61 for using appliqué shapes*

Ingredients

12oz (300ml or 345g) soya pillar blend wax
See the wick guide on page 32 to select a wick for testing
1 teaspoon (5ml) rosemary essential oil
1 teaspoon (5ml) pine essential oil
1 teaspoon (5ml) lime essential oil
Kingfisher blue and midnight blue colours
Silver appliqué wax or ready-cut wax shapes for decoration

Additional instructions

Your candle should be more than 2½in (6cm) in diameter
when using soya pillar blend wax. When set, warm the
appliqué shapes with your hands and press them onto
the candle or stick with wax glue.

Mould

Plastic pillar mould

Quantity

This recipe will make 1 candle

For centuries aromatic plant oils have been used to create incense for worship, purification and special ceremonies. Create your own tea lights with a peaceful and calming aroma to soothe your spirits.

Aromatic incense

See page 49 for instructions on making tea light candles

Ingredients

8oz (150ml or 225g) soya container wax

See the wick guide on page 32 to select a wick for testing

½ teaspoon (2.5ml) lavender essential oil

½ teaspoon (2.5ml) patchouli essential oil

¼ teaspoon (1.25ml) frankincense

10 drops (0.5ml) camphor essential oil

Aubergine and lavender colours

Moulds and containers

Metal or plastic cups and tea light holders

Quantity

This recipe will make approx. 9 tea lights

Warm, rich oranges and reds create a cosy atmosphere, with the addition of spicy oils and a crackling wood wick this flame is sure to make you glow. Pull on your woolly socks, snuggle by the fire and soak up this sizzling scent.

Winter warmer

See pages 46–48 for instructions on making container candles

Ingredients

16oz (400ml or 460g) soya container wax
See the wick guide on page 32 to select a wick for testing (the level of crackle will depend on your mix of fragrance and wax)
1 tablespoon (15ml) sweet orange essential oil
1 teaspoon (5ml) cinnamon essential oil
Orange or red colour
Dried fruit and spices for decoration

Additional instructions

Use hot glue to apply dried fruit and spices to the outside of your candle jar

Container

Kilner, apothecary, storage or preserve jar

Quantity

This recipe will make 1 candle

Follow the spice route and discover the secrets of the ancient Egyptians, Romans, Arabs and Asians. For centuries they traded their exotic commodities such as aromatic plants, herbs and spices across the continents.

Ancient secrets

See pages 46–48 for instructions on making container candles

Ingredients

26½oz (650ml or 750g) soya container wax
See the wick guide on page 32 to select a wick for testing
1 tablespoon (15ml) white musk candle fragrance oil
1 tablespoon (15ml) exotic spice candle fragrance oil
Chocolate brown and orange colours

Containers
Silver chalices

Quantity
This recipe will make approximately 3 candles

Other ideas
Why not read the history (page 11) and perfume (page 81) sections to learn more about ancient aromas and spices and make your own 'ancient secret' fragrance.

There is nothing like a walk in an ancient forest to give you a strengthening, grounded feeling. Pine is said to energize your senses, clear your mind, nose and sinuses and help relieve breathing conditions.

Spruce yourself up

See page 29 for instructions on making rubber moulds and page 42 for using them

Ingredients

8oz (200ml or 230g) white beeswax
See the wick guide on page 32 to select a wick for testing or use a square-braided wick to match your candle's diameter
1 teaspoon (5ml) pine essential oil
1 teaspoon (5ml) cedarwood essential oil
Cocoa brown colour

Additional instructions

If using soya pillar blend wax instead of beeswax, make sure that your candle is more than 2½in (6cm) in diameter.

Mould

Homemade mould using liquid latex rubber

Quantity

This recipe will make 1 candle

There is nothing like the smell of freshly fallen snow with snowflakes twinkling in the weak winter sunshine. If you can't make the ski slopes this year, make your own snowballs for a seasonal display.

Snowballs

See pages 40–41 for instructions on making pillar candles and page 54 for whipped topping and mini snowballs

Ingredients

8oz (200ml or 230g) soya pillar blend wax (base)

10½oz (300ml or 300g) soya pillar blend wax

See the wick guide on page 32 to select wicks for testing

2 teaspoons (10ml) cold water fragrance oil (base)

1 tablespoon (15ml) cold water fragrance oil (topping)

White (or no colour)

Candle glitter for decoration

Additional instructions

Make a round pillar candle. Make whipped wax and place over it. Roll leftovers into balls and pierce with a wicking pin to make hole for wick. Mini snowballs must be more than 2½in (6cm) in diameter when using soya pillar blend. Add candle glitter.

Mould

Round plastic candle mould for large candle

Quantity

This recipe makes 1 large candle and 2–3 mini candles

Candles have been used in ceremonies, festivals and celebrations for centuries and a wedding is a perfect time to light a romantic candle. For a personalized touch, make your own candle table centrepieces.

Wedding candle

See page 29 for instructions on making rubber moulds and page 42 for using them

Ingredients

12oz (300ml or 345g) white beeswax
See the wick guide on page 32 to select a wick for testing or use a square-braided wick to match your candle's diameter
1 tablespoon (15ml) orchid candle fragrance oil

Note: Make sure you fully test your candles for important or special occasions.

Additional instructions

If you decide to use soya pillar blend wax instead of beeswax, make sure that your mould is more than 2½in (6cm) in diameter. Decorate with glitter or lacquer (see pages 63–64).

Mould

Pretty silicone rubber mould with intricate detail

Quantity

This recipe makes 1 candle

Float these pretty multicoloured candles in a glass bowl with other summer flower heads. They make an attractive addition to a summer party, wedding or celebration table. Breathe in the delicate scent and let your mind float away.

Float away

See page 56 for instructions on making floating candles

Ingredients

6oz (150ml or 170g) soya pillar blend wax
See the wick guide on page 32 to select a wick for testing
1½ teaspoon (7.5ml) buttercup (or other floral) candle fragrance oil
Various, mixed colours

Moulds

Flower floating candle moulds

Additional instructions

With a spoon, scoop up a little wax of each colour and dribble into the next mould to achieve a multicoloured effect.

Quantity

This recipe will make approx. 6 candles

Use your imagination and create your own cordon bleu desserts, tarts, pastries or muffins. Use fruit-shaped ice cube moulds, coloured sheets of beeswax or appliqué wax to add culinary decorations to your masterpieces.

Chocolate cake

See page 58 for making fruit embeds, page 43 for making candles from juice cartons and page 54 for making whipped wax

Ingredients

12oz (300ml or 345g) soya pillar blend wax for the base
6oz (150ml or 170g) soya pillar blend wax for the topping
1¼oz (30ml or 35g) soya pillar blend wax for the strawberries
A small piece of brown beeswax sheet cut into tiny pieces
See the wick guide on page 32 to select a wick for testing
1 tablespoon (15ml) chocolate fudge fragrance oil (base)
1 teaspoon (5ml) non-discolouring vanilla fragrance oil (top)
Cocoa brown and red colour

Additional instructions

Make fruit embeds and leave to set. Make the base with the brown colour leaving a long wick. Put whipped wax on top of the square base leaving ¼–½in (0.5–1cm) of wick exposed at the top. Press fruit and pieces of beeswax into the soft wax.

Mould

Juice carton for base and fruit ice cube mould for fruit

Quantity

This recipe will make 1 candle

Recapture the relaxing aroma of your favourite spa. Let yourself unwind as you recall the wonderful mix of essential oils that filled the air after your pampering treatment, leaving you peaceful, refreshed and balanced.

Relaxing spa

See pages 46–48 for instructions on making container candles

Ingredients

16oz (400ml or 460g) soya container wax

See the wick guide on page 32 to select a wick for testing

(or two smaller wicks if using a container larger than 4in/10cm)

1 teaspoon (5ml) lavender essential oil

1 teaspoon (5ml) rose geranium essential oil

1 teaspoon (5ml) rosemary essential oil

½ teaspoon (2.5ml) chamomile essential oil

½ teaspoon (2.5ml) ylang ylang essential oil

Turquoise colour

Sea shells (or sea-washed glass) to decorate

Additional instructions

Add sea shells to the bottom of the container and fill with wax.

Container

Storage jar

Quantity

This recipe will make 1 candle

When you are sniffly, sneezy and all bunged up, light one of these strongly scented candles. With your tissues in one hand and hot cocoa in the other, slowly breathe in the menthol aroma.

Don't be nosey

See pages 46–48 for instructions on making container candles

Ingredients

8oz (200ml or 230g) soya container wax
See the wick guide on page 32 to select a wick for testing
½ teaspoon (2.5ml) eucalyptus essential oil
½ teaspoon (2.5ml) rosemary essential oil
½ teaspoon (2.5ml) peppermint essential oil
½ teaspoon (2.5ml) tea tree essential oil
Atlantic blue and fuchsia pink colours

Moulds

Clean, empty small tuna fish cans, thoroughly washed in hot soapy water to remove the labels

Quantity

This recipe will make 3 candles

Put your old garden pots to good use and help keep those bugs at bay. Insects do not like citrus scents and lighting one of these outdoor candles near your picnic table may make them think twice before dining with you.

Completely potty

See pages 46-48 for instructions on making container candles

Ingredients

22oz (550ml or 630g) soya container wax
See the wick guide on page 32 to select a wick for testing
(or use two smaller wicks if using a container larger than
4in/10cm)
1 tablespoon (15ml) lemongrass essential oil
2 teaspoons (10ml) citronella essential oil
Green colour

Additional instructions

If your container has a hole in the bottom, fix a pebble over the hole with hot glue, glue dot or wax glue.

Container

Extra large garden pot. For a smaller, less expensive candle use a smaller plant pot, garden urn, or preserve jar

Quantity

This recipe will make 1 large candle

A rolled beeswax candle for each of the chakra energy centres. Light a coloured candle, close your eyes and meditate, visualizing the part of the body that corresponds with the chakra colour (see chakra charts on page 87).

The bee's knees

See page 52 for instructions on making rolled beeswax candles

Ingredients
7 coloured sheets of beeswax (red, orange, yellow, green, blue, indigo and violet) each cut to 3¾in x 8in (10cm x 20cm)
Wick: No. 1 (½in) square-braided wick

Additional instructions
Make sure that the beeswax sheets are at room temperature so that they are pliable. They will not need extra fragrance as they naturally smell of beeswax and are already coloured.

Quantity
This recipe will make 7 candles

Suppliers

Many pharmacies and health food shops supply essential oils. However, you will need to purchase your wax and wicks from a candle ingredients supplier. The following are a list of mail order/ internet-based companies and the addresses provided are their trading addresses. These are warehouses and are not necessarily open to the public unless specified.

UK

4Candles UK

Tel: +44 (0)871 200 2087

www.4candles.co.uk

Extensive range of candlemaking supplies from hobby to professional, including melters and containers. Huge range of wicks including wood wicks and an excellent wick guide

E. H. Thorne (Beehives) Ltd

Tel: +44 (0)1673 858555

www.thorne.co.uk

Shop and website for beekeepers. A huge range of both amateur and professional candlemaking equipment – melters, moulds, glitters, transfers etc., beeswax and soya wax

FullMoons Cauldron

Tel: +44 (0)1344 627 945

www.fullmoons-cauldron.co.uk

All candlemaking supplies, extensive decorating materials, containers, budget and professional moulds and liquid latex for making your own moulds

Soap Basics

Tel: +44 (0)1225 899286

www.soapbasics.co.uk

Candlemaking supplies and a good range of candle glitters and metallic overdips

The British Wax Refining Co. Ltd

Tel: +44 (0)1737 761242 / 761812

www.britishwax.com

Suppliers of soya wax and beeswax

The Soap Kitchen

Tel: +44 (0)1805 622944

www.thesoapkitchen.co.uk

Huge range of candle fragrances and essential oils, soya wax, moulds and wicks

US

Bitter Creek Candle Supply, Inc.
Tel: +1-715-278-3900
www.candlesupply.com
All candlemaking supplies

Bitter Creek South Candle & Soap Supply, Inc.
Tel: +1-281-277-4440
www.bittercreeksouth.com
All candlemaking supplies

Candles and Supplies.com, Inc.
Tel: +1-215-538-8552
www.candlesandsupplies.com
Literally everything you need to make candles and more. Ingenious gadgets, melting pots, glitters, thermometers and technical support

CandleScience
Tel: +1-888-266-3916
www.candlescience.com
Huge range of candlemaking ingredients, moulds and equipment. Excellent wick guide

Nature's Garden
Tel: +1-440-647-0100
www.naturesgardencandles.com
Most candlemaking supplies

Nature's Gifts International
Tel: +1-866-573-4790
www.ngiwax.com
Producers of soya waxes. Information about soya wax plus technical support and details of their stockists. You can buy large quantities of wax direct or view their list of distributors

Peak Candle Supplies
Tel: +1-303-420-3911
www.peakcandle.com
All candlemaking supplies

Canada

Canwax
Tel: +1-905-670-6002
www.canwax.com
Everything you will need to make soya candles with wick guides. Showroom is open Tuesday to Friday

Wicks & Wax
Tel: +1-604-294-1232
www.wicksandwax.com
All candlemaking supplies

Australia & New Zealand

Aussie Candle Supplies
Tel: +61 (0)8-9249-7447
www.aussiecandlesupplies.com.au
All candlemaking supplies, with an extensive range of glass containers

Natural Candle Supply Pty Ltd
Tel: +61 (0)2-9666-8166
www.naturalcandlesupply.com.au
All candlemaking supplies including melters and thermometers

New Zealand Candle Supplies
Tel: +64 (0)9-537-2530
www.nzcandlesupplies.co.nz
Most of the supplies that you will need to start candlemaking

About the author

Elaine Stavert formed The Littlecote Soap Co. after a life-changing move from her television career in London to a farm in the beautiful Buckinghamshire countryside. Surrounded by hedgerows and meadows, and with a keen interest in herbalism and aromatherapy, Elaine was soon developing a range of natural toiletries, bath products and candles that were eco-friendly and quintessentially English. Elaine's passion for her products is evident in the pure and natural ingredients that are used in imaginative ways to produce traditional recipes with contemporary twists.

The Littlecote Soap Co.
Littlecote Farm
Littlecote
Nr Dunton
Buckingham
MK18 3LN
www.littlecotesoap.co.uk

Author's Acknowledgements

Robert, Diane and Pearl
For love, encouragement and support.

I would also like to thank my wonderful team at The Littlecote Soap Co., Caroline Heron, Nikki Jellis, Rebecca Gulliver, Andrea Ellis, Carole Capel, Jess Bliss and Diane Winks, for their hard work and dedication and for the use of their hands in the book. My thanks also to all those at Littlecote Farm; Alison Vinter in the office, Sean Jackman and Mr Nab for their sense of humour and for introducing me to a whole new array of natural aromas. Richard Phillips from The Soap Kitchen, Rob Case-Green from British Wax, Daniel and Rosemary Cap from Nature's Gifts International and Lisa Wright from The Polkadot Gallery for their help and advice. And finally to Benjamin Hedges from J. Hedges and Sons for reminding us of traditional values and without whom the company would not exist.

My grateful thanks also to the talented team at GMC Publishing, for Jonathan Bailey and Gerrie Purcell for inviting me to write this book, to Gilda Pacitti and Rob Janes for their creative eye for detail and design, Emma Foster for picture research and much more, and editors Virginia Brehaut and Sarah Doughty for their skill, professionalism and patience.

Photographic acknowledgements

Main project photography by Laurel Guilfoyle

Step-by-step photography by Elaine Stavert and also on pages: 10, 14, 15, 16, 74, 76 (middle and right), 77 (left and middle), 78 and 79 (left)

All other photography by Anthony Bailey, except as below:

Christopher Bibb: page 11 (top right)
Flickr: page 13 Temari 09 (top left) and Fotodawg (bottom right), page 17 southerntabitha (top left) and page 80 acfou
Michael Bevens: page 76 (right)
NGI Wax: page 17 (bottom right)
Rebecca Mothersole: pages 20–23, 25, 26, 27 (top), 28, 37 (top right) and 64 (left and bottom left)
Robert Stavert: page 51 (bottom left and bottom right)
Stock.xchng: page 11 kate709 (bottom left) and SEPpics (bottom right), page 12 przemeko and page 13 mooncat

Index

Names of recipes are given in italics